Monkey Titty Babies

Growing Up on St. Simons Island

Sandy + Claudia,
    Very Nice meeting ya'll,
            Sincerely
                Carol

Carol Hamby Heffernan

Carol Hamby

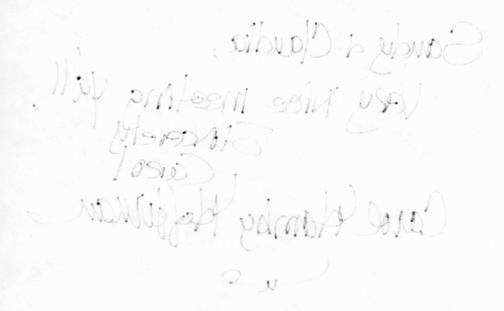

ISBN: 1499378793
ISBN 13: 9781499378795
Library of Congress Control Number: 2014908540
CreateSpace Independent Publishing Platform
North Charleston, South Carolina

Retreat Plan[s]

Hawkins Island
Broadway - p42
Frederica Rd- 4 bars - p
Golden Isles Club
Wayside Grill
The Oasis
Petes Place
Ocean Blvd - p55   elementary school
Okenfenokee Swamp - near Waycross - p60

Fort Frederica - p61
Christ Church - p61

*To my mother, **Grace,**
whose love and faith
harbored her family
through every storm
and to my daughter, **Gayle,**
whose courage, joy, and spirit
remain with me always.*

First African Baptist Church p61

Island Art Center - at airport - p64

Beachview Lighthouse — p67
Neptune Pk - p67
Casino - p67
theater - p69

Mallery - Trade Winds Cafe, Palmer St Diner,
bank, Robertas, Wards Drug
Store, Strother Hardware
Queens Court Hotel - p70

Chapter 1

LIBERTY SHIPS

The Japanese had bombed Pearl Harbor on December 7, 1941. The United States and Great Britain declared war on Japan the next day. Hitler made his declaration of war with the United States on the eleventh of December. The world was now at war.

Those of my uncles, who hadn't already enlisted, joined the military along with thousands of brave men and women. Daddy, with a wife and three children, was over enlistment age, but he served our country alongside the people who worked here at home in factories and plants. It was an intense time of sacrifice, change, and movement.

My parents, Bill and Grace Hamby, gathered up their sleeping children just before sunrise in the summer of 1942. Along with all their belongings, they loaded Betty (seven years old), Vera (three), and W.A. (one) into the backseat of our 1936 Ford sedan. I wasn't born yet, or they'd have had to squeeze me in up front. Our car rolled down the red clay driveway through early-morning ground fog, until Daddy turned onto the road toward Marietta. From there he took Highway 341 south to St. Simons Island.

Mother was worried about the accommodations that Daddy had arranged for the family to live in. He'd done that a month ago when he came to Brunswick to apply for the job at the shipyard. Would the cottage be big enough? He said it was cozy, but just how cozy was her concern. What would the neighborhood be like, and the lake out front that he couldn't stop talking about—how would she keep W.A. from falling in? Despite her worries, the prospect of living on an island dotted with palm trees and having the ocean nearby left her feeling more excitement with every mile they went.

So far the trip was going quite well. The sun was up now, and so were the children. By the time they were just south of Atlanta, the children began to get restless and complained, "Mamma, we're too hot". That was when the engine started overheating. Daddy pulled into a Stuckey's pecan stand, where they had breakfast and let the car cool down. After their meal he checked the fan belt and filled a water jug to take on the road in case the engine overheated again. With everyone fed and happy, they piled back into the car and were on their way.

The road was rough and bumpy, and sweat rolled off the kids' foreheads. Thank goodness for the breeze that came through the windows. For miles and miles, they drove past endless fields of cotton; black and white pickers worked side by side, wearing straw hats to protect themselves from the sun, and filled their canvas bags with bolls of cotton.

When the engine overheated again, Daddy pulled off the road into a large shady area behind parked wagons full of cotton. The children ran around while Mother prepared a picnic meal. After lunch they all piled back into the car and continued the long journey.

Now they began to pass miles of peach groves. Peach stands appeared up and down the highway at almost every farm entrance. When they reached Fort Valley, Daddy stopped at a gas station, hoping a mechanic could look at the car, but there wasn't anybody available, so he bought some gas and filled the jug with more water. Every forty or fifty miles, the car overheated again. Daddy was getting more and more frustrated; and Mother was coming unhinged because of these uncontrollable, rowdy children and the fear they would be stranded in the middle of nowhere on the side of a sweltering highway.

After 350 miles and almost twelve hours on the road, they finally came to a sign that read *US 17 south to Brunswick/St. Simons*. Hooray! What a huge relief! A few miles later, Daddy turned onto the causeway to St. Simons

Island. "We're almost there!" he said. That's when that darn car overheated again. One more time, Daddy pulled off the road to cool down the engine.

Mother and the children sat on the running board of the car gazing at the sunset. It was unbelievably beautiful. The sky, brilliant red and orange, made the marsh grasses glow like flames of fire. On either side of the car rabbits hopped out from the marsh and nibbled on the roadside grass. A cool breeze from the ocean refreshed everyone and the long hot ride in the steamy old car was nearly forgotten.

"Grace," my daddy said, "this is paradise!"

Daddy came to St. Simons to work in the shipyard for J.A. Jones Construction Company, where he helped build Liberty ships. These cargo vessels of the sea were vital for transporting materials to troops in Europe and the Pacific.

Daddy had rented a cottage in Glynn Haven Motor Court, a neighborhood located in the middle of the island that was owned by Dan Cowart. "Just Mine Cottage" overlooked a small freshwater lake. It was pea sized, with two bedrooms and a kitchenette. Mother wasn't sure they could live in such tight quarters; it was going to be hard, but there was nothing else available.

All of the cottages sat close to the edge of the water, and a dirt road, which circled the lake, went past the front of the cottages. Cars and trail riders from Sea Island Stables frequently went by. The lake was full of fish, turtles, and the odd snake, and tourists could rent small boats from Mr. Cowart.

Dan Cowart also owned and ran a general store on Frederica Road at the entrance to the motor court. If anyone asked him how he was, he'd answer, "Mighty fine, mighty fine. Wonderful world. All is well." That was how he got his nickname, Mighty Fine. He was a rotund, jolly man who wore suspenders and resembled Santa Claus. Every year, just before Christmas, Mighty Fine drove his flashy Kaiser automobile down to Florida and filled it to the brim with fruits and nuts. When he returned to Glynn Haven, he'd deliver them to the neighborhood children.

Mighty Fine was quite the entrepreneur. He owned hundreds of acres of land on St. Simons, as well as other businesses. But his arch nemesis and greatest competitor was Mr. Andrews, who owned Andrews Grocery. He too was a very good businessman. Mr. Andrews's store was only a couple of blocks away from Mighty Fine's, and if you couldn't find something at Dan's store, you'd go to Andrews Grocery. Mr. Andrews was a butcher and gave credit to black and white customers alike. Both of these men were very popular with everyone. Their stores were where everyone gathered to keep up with the events going on with the war.

Mother and Daddy had met lots of people in the community and they were beginning to feel more at home on the lake. But, living on the lake almost became a tragedy on the day Mother had the life scared out of her. Our screen door was accidentally left unlatched, and W.A. had wandered off. Mother ran out the back door, screaming frantically. The neighbors all came running and offered to help search for him. Finally they found him playing at the edge of the lake in the water. Mother was horrified. Grabbing him in her arms, she vowed they would find another place to live. It wasn't going to be easy; more than fifteen thousand workers had recently come to the area to build ships, and they needed housing too. Men and women—black and white—worked in the shipyard. Merchants of all descriptions, as well as doctors, nurses, lawyers, and other professionals inflated the population to more than forty thousand. Housing was in extremely short supply. It was so bad, local people turned their homes into boardinghouses. They rented beds out by shifts. One tenant would sleep in a bed and then leave for an eight-hour shift at the shipyard. The owner would then change the bed linens for the next tenant to come home and sleep. Some workers had to live and sleep in their cars.

Daddy didn't want to leave the lake, but Mother was determined to move to a safer location. They eventually found and purchased two lots on Broadway near the airport. Mother said it would be an ideal place to raise the kids. The bank loaned them money for purchasing the lots but would not give them a construction loan.

Mother quickly realized that getting enough money to start construction was going to be almost impossible unless she went to work. A neighbor who was a nurse at the Brunswick hospital told her of a training program for nurses. If Mother was interested, the neighbor would recommend her to the program directors. After hours of pleading with Daddy, Mother started training in the emergency room at the Brunswick hospital. Daddy had to keep the children at night while she worked.

Soon, they had enough money to start building the house. Everything was in short supply during the war. I mean everything. Daddy had to use the black market to get copper pipe, nails, and so many other materials. He haggled for this and traded for that, and there were times when Mother thought he'd never finish. But after two years the house was finally ready.

To add to the excitement, Mother became pregnant with me. I was born on June 11, 1944, in the Brunswick hospital. It was only a week or two after my birth that they moved into the new house. Some workers had just poured a sidewalk, so Mother and Daddy pressed my feet into the concrete and dated it. In the years that followed, I often made a point of comparing my feet to those first tiny footprints.

After a few months, Daddy was injured at the shipyard. A piece of steel fell off the scaffolding and landed on his foot. He told us that when he removed his boot and sock, his big toe fell onto the ground. A big black cat scooted out from nowhere. He grabbed the toe as if it were a mouse and ran off with it. He ate Daddy's toe. That's why they never sewed it back on.

Daddy left the shipyard to become a mechanic at the naval air base. He found another job because his boss told him that he needed to have both big toes to work in the shipyard. Whenever he changed his shoes and socks, we children would say, "Daddy, tell us the story about the cat and your toe." Was it a true story? Who knows? But we loved it.

$Chapter\ 2$

THE NANCY HANKS TRAIN

*E*very spring Mother made us new clothes for our annual trip to her family's Decoration Day. Daddy drove Mother, Betty, Vera, W.A., and me to Savannah, where we caught the Nancy Hanks train to Atlanta. This was no ordinary steam engine. The Nancy Hanks was a beautiful new passenger train named after a famous racehorse that had been named in honor of Abraham Lincoln's mother. I was very proud to be riding on a train that shared the name of Abraham Lincoln's mother. This was one of the most exciting times of my youth.

When we arrived at the station carrying our bags, we entered a huge, grand terminal. I can still feel the excitement of boarding that bright blue train and walking down the middle aisle until we found our seats. The red leather passenger seats were all reserved, and it made me feel special to think we each had a seat with our name on it. Black passengers were seated in a separate section, and they were not allowed to eat at the grill in the lounge car.

As we pulled away from the station and waved good-bye to Daddy, Mother warned him to stay out of the bars. With a puff of steam and a blow of the shrill whistle, the train began chugging along. Gaining speed, it moved quickly through the countryside. A waiter came through the cars taking orders for refreshments. I loved being waited on. I couldn't stop looking through the window, which yielded a constantly changing view and opened my eyes to another world. Many of the houses we passed were shacks. I felt sad that some people had to live in houses like this. With one stop in Macon, the trip took us about six hours.

As we arrived at the elaborate Atlanta terminal, one of my mother's brothers was standing patiently, waiting to pick us up. We drove to Marietta for a short visit with my Granny Hamby and Daddy's sister, Frances, whom everyone called Sis. People always said that Sis was kind of slow. She was quiet and mousy looking, and everybody was so busy talking at each other while she seemed to fade into the corner.

Granny was a beautiful, white-haired lady who wore her hair in a bun. She sat in a large chintz upholstered chair with hand-crocheted doilies on the arms and back. She always had on her lap a red leather Bible with gold leaf lettering. It was so big it seemed to weigh her down, keeping her from floating straight up to heaven. She kept another Bible on a side table where there were stacks of religious books and articles from which she studied Scripture. Verses rolled off Granny's tongue like a biblical scroll, echoing through my ears and filling every corner of my head. But the words meant nothing to me. It was like she spoke in a foreign language. I respected Granny Hamby, but what I really wished for was to spend more time together. She was sweet and kind toward us children, but I didn't like the way she talked about Daddy.

Daddy's drinking was of grave concern to Granny. She strongly stated that his sins would rest on his children and his children's children. Her comment always confused me, because I wondered why God would make me pay for my father's sins. It seemed like an unfair thing for God to do to a child. I came to the conclusion that if Daddy would stop drinking and abusing, it would make God, Granny Hamby, and all of us happy.

Soon, with a little kiss and a pat on the head from Granny, Mother would herd us out the door. We'd then make short visits to other relatives like Uncle Gold and Aunt Olif, who lived in a rustic farmhouse not far away. You could see under their house where the dogs and chickens lay to stay cool. The roosters in the yard attacked you the minute you stepped on the ground. Screaming and running, we'd jump onto the porch and scamper into the house.

This farmhouse was very much like the one that Granny Mathis lived in as a child. It always reminded me of the stories Granny Mathis told us about Confederate and Union soldiers who came to steal food when her mother was a child. The children all hid under their house, petrified of what the soldiers might do. Sherman swept through their farms on the way to Atlanta, taking everything in sight.

As soon as we finished saying our hellos to our aunt and uncle, we immediately begged Aunt Olif to play the piano. She would prop open the screen door, sit down at the piano, and play "Some Glad Morning." Suddenly her pet carrier pigeon would fly into the house and land on top of the piano and then march back and forth to the beat of the tune.

> Some glad morning when this life is o'er,
> I'll fly away;
> To a home on God's celestial shore,
> I'll fly away (I'll fly away).
> I'll fly away, Oh Glory
> I'll fly away; (in the morning)
> When I die, Hallelujah, by and by,
> I'll fly away (I'll fly away)…

When Aunt Olif finished playing the tune, the bird would fly away, and we'd laugh our heads off. We'd retire to the parlor for refreshments, and Mother would catch up on all of the Hamby family news.

After visiting the Hamby family, we'd set off to the farm where Mother grew up and descend upon Granny and Grandpa Mathis. Their farm was a treasure chest of adventure for children. With horses, cows, pigs, sheep, and chickens to visit, tractors to ride on, and barns to play in, we couldn't have been happier if we'd gone to heaven. The two-story, pine-clapboard house was surrounded on three sides by a wide porch.

My cousin Judy and I would sit on the front-porch swing, a favorite with all the kids, where we conjured up plans that inevitably got us into trouble, though we never meant to. Trouble just happened, and somehow we ended up in the middle of it. Judy was a lovely, bubbly blonde with lots of imagination and curiosity; between my curiosity and her instigation, we were never bored. We were always fascinated by the well in the front yard, especially when the grown-ups drew water from it. But knowing our knack for getting into mischief, the grown-ups warned us to steer clear of it. We might fall in and drown, or the crank handle that brought the bucket up from the well might hit us in the head. Luckily that was one bit of trouble we didn't get into.

Granny's house was not fancy inside; everything had a practical use, and nothing was wasted. If it was too fine to sit on or too pretty to use, it wasn't likely you'd see it there. As you entered the hallway, the bedrooms were on the right and the left. Next you entered the parlor and then the dining room, which you'd walk through to get to the huge kitchen in back. A large wood-burning stove kept the kitchen warm, the water heated, and the family fed.

Mealtime revolved around Granny's rules, which had to be observed. Dishes, pots, and pans were washed and put away. You were not allowed back in the kitchen between meals. When we were hungry, my cousins and I would sneak around the house, checking to see where Granny was. Then we'd slip onto the side porch, where the huge pie safe was filled with leftovers. We'd crawl along the floor under the harvest tables, make our way to the pie safe, open it, grab pieces of fried chicken and fried pies, and then run like hell before getting caught by the strictest, tiniest, and meanest little lady known to man.

Granny was strict in many other ways. There was no running in and out of the house. You were either outside playing, or you were put to bed. And if you wanted to defy her by being in the house and hanging around, you were subject to a physical examination much like the following.

"Feeling peaked, child?" Granny said as she grabbed you. First she'd examine your eyes and your tongue, and then she'd feel your tummy. I'd look at Mother to save me, hoping that Granny wouldn't have to give me any medicine. But Granny's verdict was swift and final. No appeals.

"To bed for rest and a dose of medicine." Then she'd spoon out the most awful medicine I'd ever tasted. She would roll the feather mattress back, and slap the bed several times with her stick, not to fluff it but to intimidate you into staying in bed until she decided that your sentence was up.

Bed rest wasn't only a disciplinary measure because it was a good thing when you had a tummy ache, and I often experienced both. My tummy ache was usually brought on by my disgust with the outhouse. I'd do anything to keep from going to the outhouse, where insects in the early stages of life populated and thrived. There were maggots, flies, wasps, and worms. Mother always said, "Just don't look down in there!" How could you not look at somewhere you were about to place your butt and some of your other very important parts? I was always afraid of falling into that horrible mess!

Granny had a garden that was off-limits to the children where she grew her Cherokee herbal cures. She was well known for her remedies. Granny lived on one end of Trickum Road, and Dr. Bannister lived on the other end. It was said that she had almost as many patients as he did. After I climbed into bed with my tummy ache, Granny would give me a healthy dose of her herbal medicine. To further humiliate me, my brother and cousins would tap on the window and tease me. Their ugly little faces popped up and down, looking into the bedroom through the lace curtains. I don't know what she gave me, but it was never long before I upped my gown and grabbed my little chamber pot. The first poo would hit the pot like a bunch of marbles. Then suddenly the "big event" would happen, and I'd feel so much better. Granny gets full credit for that miracle cure.

One of the annual events at Granny Mathis's was the Chicken Feed and Flour Sack Conference, where Mother, Granny, and my mother's sisters and sisters-in-law all sat around the harvest tables sorting their chicken feed and flour sacks. These sacks, which had been collected and saved all year, were washed and pressed beforehand. First the women sorted them into bundles by pattern and color, and then the serious trading began. My mother made pillowcases and sheets with the feed sacks, and she used the printed flour sacks for clothing, tablecloths, and towels.

After this they had a War Conference. They would relive the hardships and sacrifices they had made during World War II. They'd talk about how they had to give up spending time with their children to go to work for the war effort. Many of the jobs were tedious, difficult, and exhausting, yet the women still had to return home and deal with all the household chores. Soldiers were always recognized for their war effort with ribbons, medals, and promotions in military rank, but the women's sacrifices were overlooked and unrecognized.

Mother and her sisters

The Sunday before leaving to return to St. Simons, all the family would make a pilgrimage to Jasper to attend the Stanley and Garland Decoration Day. Granny Mathis looked particularly pretty in her brightly printed dress with a lace collar and her broad-rimmed black hat and heels. The men, who were all shaved and clean in freshly starched and ironed white shirts, donned fine straw hats with silk bands. Even Mother wore a hat that Sunday. The kids had also been decked out in their best clothes to be "shown off" to the relatives. Everyone wanted to make a good impression. Decoration Day was originally started to commemorate the Union and Confederate soldiers who died during the War Between the States. It is now known as Memorial Day. We were packed into the cars so tightly we could hardly breathe. There were baskets full of fried chicken, peach and apple fried pies, and burnt-caramel cakes; American flags and dozens of handmade crepe paper flowers were stuffed in the trunks.

Upon arriving after the two-hour trip, we were greeted warmly by friends and relatives. We quickly entered the small, white-framed church for a prayer service. The single room, plain and simple as an empty shoebox, filled with the preacher's voice and our shouts of hallelujah in response. We clapped hands to the music, swayed our bodies, and made praises to the Lord. After all, we were Baptists. Tears flowed in that church like the River Jordan while each one of us memorialized our soldiers and family members who'd died and gone to the Promised Land. When the service was over, the preacher said a most appropriate blessing before we exited the church.

As soon as we stepped outside, my eyes landed on long, cloth-covered harvest tables bearing a colorful array of platters, bowls, and containers that overflowed with home-cooked, potluck vittles. I thought I had gone to heaven. After filling our tummies to a disgraceful capacity, we walked through the cemetery placing flags on the graves of soldiers—many of whom had been in the Confederate army—and flowers on our deceased loved ones' graves. The day seemed as if it lasted a week, but it was eventually time to leave. I got lots of juicy kisses that I really didn't want and hugs from some ladies who wore the worst perfume I had ever smelled. We all said our good-byes with a promise to see them next year.

Family Reunion

Granny Mathis and other relatives

The next morning Uncle Keith drove all of us to Atlanta to catch the train back to Savannah. The visit wasn't really for us kids; it was for Mother. She really enjoyed being with her family, except her sister, Beulah, who always made her mad for a variety of reasons. Beulah was constantly attacking Daddy's character, but Mother had too much class to react to her comments. Beulah made Mother feel inferior in almost every way. It was a rivalry that had gone on between them since childhood. Mother often threatened that one day she would pull Beulah's hair out. It took the entire train ride for Mother to calm down. I think that Vera and I must have slept the whole way back to Savannah, as we were always exhausted by our visit.

Chapter 3

BETTY

$\mathcal{W}$hen my older sister Betty was born, she was so tiny that Mother and Daddy brought her home in a shoebox. They were concerned that she might not live, but with my mother's tender loving care, she grew up to be a healthy child.

Betty was so pretty. She had blond hair and a shapely, athletic figure. Her loveliness and grace were evident when she smiled. She was very smart and popular in school. Her curiosity and enthusiasm were infectious. I loved watching her march and twirl her baton in parades.

One day when I was six years old, Mother was making supper when the phone rang. She picked up the phone and said hello and, a second later, let out a scream so loud that it deafened me. A friend had called to alert Mother that Betty had eloped with a guy from West Virginia. Betty was only sixteen, and this boy, Kenny, who had been visiting his cousin in our neighborhood, had only known Betty for a couple of months. We sat there wanting to know who he was. Betty should have told us about him and that she was in love with him. We were in total shock. It was so unlike Betty to do such a stupid, irrational thing.

Mother, Daddy, and I jumped into the car to try to catch her before she got off the island. Driving as fast as we could over the causeway, we went over several wooden bridges that made the boards bounce beneath the car. I was in the backseat bouncing so much that my head kept hitting the top of the car. As we barreled up US Highway 17, Mother kept saying, "Hurry. We've got to stop them."

"I'm going as fast as I can, Grace," Daddy said each time, but the car went faster anyway. After we covered about forty miles, we reached a point where we realized we could never catch them. Mother was in hysterics, Daddy was beating the steering wheel with his fist, and I started to cry.

Mother was distraught for days. Daddy was grumpy. I was very, very sad. The phone kept ringing with calls from the rest of our family, who were all just as worried and upset as we were. What stupid thing has she gone and done? None of us even knew this boy. Where did he come from? West Virginia? She'd run off with a hillbilly!

I knew deep down that she might have been in love but the real reason she ran off with this guy was that she wanted to get away from Daddy's drinking and abuse. Over time we accepted the fact that Betty had married. This was her choice. She wasn't coming back to live with us. We all missed her terribly. There was a huge void in the house.

Betty wrote to Mother every week or two. I think she was missing us too. A little more than a year passed before Betty and her new husband came back for a visit. I had missed her so much. I didn't think that the hillbilly boy was so great. He wore thick glasses and was so thin he didn't even look like a husband. He looked more like a high school kid. I was only seven, but even I could see he was bragging half the time. Kenny was the type who thought he knew everything.

My parents were still in shock, but I guess it was payback time. Mother and Daddy had run away and gotten married when she was aged sixteen and he was twenty-five. But it was not a shotgun wedding in either case. Betty seemed genuinely in love with Kenny, just as Mother was genuinely in love with Daddy.

Kenny started begging Daddy to go hog hunting. Daddy tried to explain to him that hunting wild razorback hog was a dangerous sport. They weren't just cute little pigs. He reassured Daddy that he had been hunting before and knew how to handle a gun. My father just laughed and said, "OK, I'll take you." He still didn't think this was such a good idea. Daddy hadn't recovered yet from Kenny running off with his daughter. This might give Daddy an opportunity to shoot him.

So, Daddy, Kenny, W.A., and some friends loaded up Daddy's best hounds, Big Red and Blue, into the truck and drove to Taylor's Fish Camp on the north end of the island. They let the dogs loose and started walking down a hog trail. It wasn't long before the dogs sounded. Daddy called them back to his side, for he didn't want them to get hurt by a hog. The guys walked on through the trail until they came upon a litter of grunting pigs, seemingly confused as to where to go next.

Daddy looked up as a *huge* sow approached. He said to Kenny, "Stop walking and let her pass. There are probably more sows nearby, and we don't want to disturb them. You have to be careful and do exactly what I say. Don't shoot that sow; she has babies."

Kenny paid no attention and continued walking toward the sow, taking aim, firing, and missing. Daddy said you could see the rage in that mother's eyes, and he told Kenny to just stay still. But Kenny shot again and missed. In an instant the sow was after him. She attacked his heels, her tusk ripping through his boot and pants. He started hitting her in the head with the stock of his gun. Over and over he struck her, but she was determined to protect her babies. Then the gun fell apart. By now the sow had gored his leg with her tusk and Kenny was yelling at the top of his lungs. No one could do anything to help him. He tried to outrun her and made for a pine sapling as she nipped and bit at his legs. Kenny managed to climb the tree high enough to be out of her reach. After a while the sow retreated, and she and her litter scampered back into the woods.

Daddy, W.A., and their friends laughed so hard they were holding onto one another and falling over. He said to Kenny, "Hey, hillbilly, didn't I tell you that she would eat you up?"

Kenny's leg had a bad cut on it, his pants were ripped, and his gun was now in a hundred pieces. Daddy loved to tell this story, and he always finished it by saying he missed his opportunity to shoot Kenny that day but he was glad he didn't.

Wild hog meat was an important staple at our dinner table and at many other people's on the island. The problem was in knowing how to cook it. My daddy learned to cook it from an old black man who lived on the north end. Daddy would put the hams and the shoulders into Mother's biggest pressure cooker. The odor that came from the steam was wild and gamy like dirty socks. Mother would leave the house and sit outside on the patio during this process; she couldn't stand the smell. When the steam-cooker gauge reached red, Daddy would cool it down and drain off the liquid. He'd repeat this process a couple of times. With the final cooking, he would put carrots, onions, celery, and spices in the pot. After it finished cooking, he added barbeque sauce.

That meat was so delicious it was well worth the risk of being caught by Doc Jones, the game warden. Doc Jones was always chasing after Daddy, trying to keep him from hunting hogs on private property.

Chapter 4

ELIZA AND AUGUSTA, GEORGIA, 1952–1953

My life was about to change. Mother started to get sick every day; the life was being drained out of her. She acted strange in many ways. She would not let you see her without her clothes on, even in emergencies when you needed to get into the bathroom. Mother started growing black hair on her face, arms, and legs. She tried to keep it shaved, but it was getting totally out of hand. She was gaining weight, too—lots of weight. We were suspicious that maybe she was going to have a baby.

One day I came home from school to find she had been rushed to the Medical College of Georgia in Augusta for surgery to remove tumors from her belly. We were happy to hear that she didn't have cancer, but she was put under the care of Dr. Robert Greenblatt, a French Canadian. Dr. Greenblatt was doing clinical work in reproductive endocrinology in the treatment of ovulatory disorders. Daddy said the doctor had new ideas on how to treat women with these types of problems. He explained to us that our mother had agreed to be part of his research and that, in order for her to get well, she would have to stay in the hospital for a long time.

Mother had always been the glue that held us together. Now Daddy was totally in charge, but he didn't have the skills to run a household. The housework went undone, and the laundry started piling up. We had no relatives nearby to help, and we kids were of no use. Mother had always done everything. It was her life caring for her family.

I didn't know how to cook. My father only knew how to cook grits and eggs. He did make rubber bread, his very own recipe. Sometimes Daddy's dogs wouldn't even eat it. He couldn't make individual biscuits, so he made one big pone. It was awful! He made sugar syrup out of boiled sugar, water, and butter. Rubber biscuits and sugar syrup—yuck! I would get so hungry, so I quickly learned how to cook.

Eliza

19

Weeks went by before Daddy finally said to me, "Come with me. We're going to get Eliza." We needed help badly, so we climbed into our rusty old truck and drove to the slave cabin where she lived. Eliza White was a beautiful black woman who lived in the old slave cabin with her mother, Ellen, her father, Floyd, and several other family members. Floyd and his mother, Victoria, were, like Eliza, born in this slave cabin. Floyd's father was Jupiter, a slave at Kelvin Grove Plantation. Victoria had been a slave at Retreat Plantation. Victoria and her family are listed on the estate inventory of Anna Matilda King. This was the same inventory used in the 1860 bankruptcy of the Retreat Plantation (see appendix).

I just can't fathom what it must have been like, knowing that a value was put on each and every member of your family. Anna Matilda King, according to Eliza, showed more concern for the welfare of her slaves than many other plantation owners. She provided wagons to take the slaves back and forth from their cabins to the fields. Her people were rated and assigned duties according to their ability: full hands, three-quarter hands, half hands, and quarter hands. They worked using the task system, where they were assigned specific tasks to do during the day. When they finished they had free time to work in their own gardens. Anna, on occasion, used the gang system on her plantation. Most of the other plantations on the island used the gang system where slaves would work in large groups under supervision of black or white slave drivers

Retreat Plantation had a two-story hospital made of tabby, a building material made from oyster shells, lime, and sand. It was a large, eight-room building with attic space and windows that went from floor to ceiling. Women slaves were assigned as nurses and midwives. When a doctor was needed, one was summoned from the mainland.

Eliza's father kept a large vegetable garden behind their cabin. He'd often pick a mess of greens and give them to Eliza to cook for us while she worked in our house. Eliza cooked the best greens, with the smoky flavor of a ham hock making the pot liquor—nectar of the gods. Next to their garden were the cotton fields where watermelon vines rambled across the sandy soil. It is my understanding that watermelon seeds came here in the pockets of slaves from Africa. Scattered throughout the yard and garden was a variety of chickens. Not all of the chickens were for human consumption. One type called a frizzle chicken was there to dig up any wudu (voodoo) or spells buried there by their enemy. Herbs, roots, or hair would be buried in the path so that when the victim walked on it, he or she got the curse.

The slave cabin where they lived was a one-and-a-half-story tabby building that had originally housed two families. Inside, part of the wall had been cut away so that their family could use the entire cabin.

Daddy and I entered the back door on the right-hand side and stepped onto the wide plank floors made of solid pine. A double fireplace in the middle of the house had been whitewashed but was dirty from the soot. Two oak rockers flanked the hearth. There were staircases on either end of the rooms that led up to a sleeping area. Exposed ceiling rafters supported the upstairs floor. A smaller room on the right contained a table and chairs and a wood-burning cook stove. Small windows cast light into the rooms, just enough for me to read the newspapers that had been glued to the walls. They were yellowed with age and had obviously been printed many years before. I remember laughing at the advertisements for things I had never heard of and at the funny clothes people wore in the photos. I asked why they had newspapers on the walls, and it was explained to me that it kept the haunts or ghosts busy reading the papers so that they wouldn't bother you. It worked. It kept me busy while Eliza got her things. Eliza and her family had strong faith in wudu, curses, and spells.

After Eliza got her things, we would stop at the gasoline station across the road and get a treat: Coca-Cola and peanuts for Eliza and Nehi Orange and moon pies for me. In the heat of summer, it was refreshing to search for your drink in the big red cooler with huge chunks of ice floating around. But if you took too long, you would freeze your hand off. Daddy paid for the treats then Eliza and I would go laughing and giggling back to the truck. We all hopped into the truck for a short drive to Broadway and to the filthiest house on St. Simons.

The first job Eliza tackled was to strip the beds and start washing the sheets. Our washing machine was outside on a concrete slab next to Daddy's shop. Eliza would then hang them on the clothesline, and my brother would tease her. Sometimes he would stand on the other side of the wet sheet, put his hands out, and act like he was a ghost. It terrified her. Other times he would chase her, trying to put a snake or lizard on her. I can see her now running through the wet clothes on the clothesline yelling, "You are the meanest child I've ever known. You devil child!" W.A. just loved it.

The next thing she did was mop the floors barefoot. Eliza had webbed toes. She would soap up the kitchen floor and start patting her feet, making bubbles. She'd do a jig, jumping and dancing around the room singing, "Poor little Liza, little Liza Jane." She would hold my hands while shuffling. We would slip, slide, and dance around the kitchen table, laughing our heads off. Eliza said that she was a professional dancer because she danced for money. She and the other children would do a jig in front of the slave cabin for the tourists as they went by. Her daddy would put a hat on the steps so that the tourists could drop money into it.

Eliza certainly was a blessing to all of us. Being the youngest, I especially needed her. She constantly assured me that Mother was going to be OK and that she would be coming home real soon. Lots of hugs and laughs made it bearable.

She could easily have made more money working for some rich folk on Sea Island, but instead she chose to work for us. We didn't have very much money to pay her—only a few dollars—but we'd give her fish from the freezer and home-canned vegetables. I believe that our love for each other made it worthwhile to her.

After weeks and weeks, Mother finally came home. She continued to take her hormone medicine and make trips to Augusta to see Dr. Greenblatt. She was photographed, month after month and then year after year, as part of research that was published in medical journals. This research led to the monthly oral contraceptive that came out in 1966. She was also one of the first to have a hormone pellet implant put into her abdomen. Mother lost all of her abnormal facial and body hair.

With Eliza's help, Mother was back to her old self, and we all settled into our old routine. Yes, even Daddy was good for a while, but all too soon he went back to drinking.

Chapter 5

MONKEY TITTIES

Our family at Christmas

few weeks before Christmas, Eliza and Mother would go to the Community Market at The Pier and buy what they needed for Christmas baking. When they came in the door with their bags of groceries, Eliza would be giggling and excited to tell us that she had monkey titties for us. "Come and sit at the table so we can make monkey titty babies." Eliza then pulled brown, fuzzy coconuts out of the bag and laid them on the table. Mother let us pick out material from her stack of flour sacks in the bedroom, and we'd use these to wrap our babies in. Then where the three indented places were on the coconut, we'd color in the eyes with blue crayons and the lips with red. They now had faces and with their brown fuzzy hair were so cute.

I think the idea for the dolls came from Eliza—maybe something from her African heritage. These coconuts became our beloved wards for the next two weeks. We played with our babies so much that they eventually lost all of their hair. The only thing that ruined our fun was W.A. He was a real nuisance. He would steal or hide our monkey titty babies. He'd toss them in the air and roll them on the floor so hard against the furniture that we thought he'd break them. I'd yell at my brother and scream at the top of my lungs, afraid he was going to destroy my little monkey baby. But W.A. just laughed and kept doing whatever he could to get a rise out of us girls. He got such a thrill out of picking on us. He was a real brat.

Near Christmas Day Mother would inform us that we had to hand over our monkey babies. Sighing, we'd reluctantly hand them over. She'd get a clean dish towel, a hammer, and an ice pick. Then we'd be really upset because we knew the fate of our babies. We'd follow Mother out to the back door's concrete steps, where she took a coconut, one at a time, and, using an ice pick, poked out the baby's eyes and then its mouth, draining the coconut milk into a bowl. Then she'd wrap the coconut in the clean dish towel, lay it on the concrete step, and strike it with the hammer, breaking it into several pieces. It was a big drama as we moaned and groaned through what we thought was an execution of our babies.

"Oh my Lord, my poor baby is gone!" Collecting our emotions, we'd go back into the kitchen, where we sat at the table as Mother trimmed the pieces of coconut. She'd hand each one of us a nice big chunk to make up for the loss of our babies. While we ate, Eliza grated a huge pile of snow-white coconut. It smelled so good. Mother and Eliza would then start to make coconut cream pies and a coconut cake. We just couldn't wait for Christmas dinner to enjoy these yummy desserts.

Once when she was baking, one of us asked, "Eliza, why are you so brown?" She told us that God had left her in the oven too long. We laughed. We'd ask her this all the time after that, and she'd tell us the same thing and comment that we're all God's children and he bakes us at different temperatures. There was something comforting about Eliza's answer.

After all of the Christmas baking was completed, it was time for Daddy to take his boat to Hawkins Island and cut our Christmas tree. Sometimes when he arrived home with the tree, it was a disappointment, because cedars don't make the best Christmas trees. Mother had a great talent for taking a sad little tree and making it look beautiful. She would take extra limbs, wiring them up and down the trunk, and make the tree look thicker. She put the lights on, and then we put all the other decorations on the tree. Mother was a real stickler about the icicles being hung on the tree one at a time. No cheating! It would always turn out beautiful.

Daddy also brought home huge branches of mistletoe and cassina holly. Lots of mistletoe grew in the trees on Hawkins Island. All Daddy would do was shoot his gun into the tree several times, and the mistletoe would fall to the ground. He'd cut large bunches of the holly with his knife. Mother always put the cassina holly in a large container on the table that sat on our front porch. She'd take the mistletoe, tie a red ribbon around it, and hang it over the front door. We had so much fun pouncing on people and trying to kiss them (especially boys, who hated it) as they came in the house.

W.A.

We didn't get a lot of gifts. Some years there were more than others. Mother would wrap all the gifts and put them under the tree. W.A. would snoop. He'd even unwrap gifts—like a football—and play with them and then wrap them up again like nothing had ever happened. I'm sure Mother was aware of what he was doing. Santa had to bring W.A. a bicycle every year because he'd trashed the one he got the year before. The bike was his main means of transportation around the island. He'd always get some type of gun too, like a BB gun or a rifle. But Mother always stressed that Christmas wasn't all about gifts; it was about Lord Jesus.

Mother's greatest wish was that Daddy wouldn't spend all his paycheck at the bars—he liked to buy drinks for all the boys at Pete's—and that he would be sober over the Christmas holidays. The holiday season was usually the start of a binge. My father was the stupidest man. He never bought Mother a personal gift. It was always something like a stove, a fridge, or something else for the kitchen. All she really wanted was for him to stay sober.

The most exciting thing was Christmas Eve. Each year Santa arrived at The Pier in a boat at about six o'clock, got on the fire truck, and started circling the island. We'd be sitting in the living room on the sofa listening for the fire truck's siren. Once we heard it in the distance, off we'd go in a rush through the front door, down the sidewalk, and into the street, yelling.

"He's here! He's here!" Our eyes were fixed on Demere Road where it crossed ours, far down the street. Suddenly the fire engine would go by in a flash. You could see Santa sitting on top of the truck. His red arm and white-gloved hand waved as they roared down the road. We jumped up and down with joy and then turned quickly, yelling, "Hurry, Mother. We have to beat him back down to The Pier."

She laughed. "Get into the car." We quickly packed into the car along with all the neighborhood kids. Mother never drove fast enough to please us. "Hurry! Hurry!" we yelled.

After parking the car, we ran like crazy to get lined up at the big Christmas tree in front of the library at The Pier. We couldn't wait to get our Christmas stocking. When Santa arrived in the fire truck with the siren blasting, it put the children into a state of total excitement. He climbed down from the fire truck, came over to where we children were standing, and handed out the stockings. After we all got our stockings, we piled into the car to go back home and began to eat our Christmas goodies. Chaos broke out as we fought over one another's stockings, which always contained an apple, an orange, a candy cane, and a small prize.

"Mother, W.A. took my apple!"

"Well, you can't have my apple!"

Negotiations continued all the way home. The smell of peppermint filled the car as we munched on our candy canes. We could hardly contain our excitement about seeing Santa and knowing that Christmas Eve was finally here. When we got back from The Pier, there in the kitchen, sitting at the table, was Daddy with his head in his hands looking at his bottle of Old Crow or some other rot-gut whiskey. He cried like a baby. "Grace, I thought you left me. Where have you been?"

"You stupid fool. We were at The Pier seeing Santa. If you had come home instead of being at Pete's bar, you would have known. You could have gone with us."

One Christmas Eve Vera locked our bedroom door to keep me from coming in. My mother said, "Carol, don't bother your sister. She's making something really special for you." I couldn't wait to see this special gift that she was making.

On Christmas morning, we were excited as we opened our gifts. I spotted Vera's beautifully wrapped gift and opened it. I took a long stare at it. Would you believe Vera had taken matchboxes, glued them together, covered them with paper, made little knobs, and put little prizes that came out of Cracker Jack boxes in each of the little drawers? I thought, "Is this what she spent all of this time working on? This big secret? What—this is *it*?" Well, I threw *it* down and quickly picked up my new baby doll that Santa had brought me. Suddenly I was hanging in midair. My mother had snatched me up and proceeded to march me into the bedroom.

"Carol, you have hurt your sister's feelings. It is not the price of the gift but the thought put into it. Now you go back in there and tell her you like her gift."

Holding back my tears, I was so ashamed of myself. From then on I was always sensitive to my sister's feelings.

That same morning Daddy handed Mother a white envelope. She opened it and looked around at each and every one of us and smiled. We had no idea of what it was. Had Daddy just given Mother another new refrigerator?

"What is it, Mother?"

"It's a payment book."

"A payment book? For what?"

"A television!"

We jumped up and down, yelling screams of delight enough to deafen anyone nearby. We may have been the last people in the neighborhood to get a television. Daddy assured us that though it was a long time coming, ours was going to be the biggest and the best. This gift from Daddy made all of us very happy. I think Mother forgave him this time for giving her one more appliance.

That afternoon we kids insisted that Daddy connect our new television. He had just finished off a bottle of whiskey, and as he walked out to the backyard, he threw the empty bottle under the house. He went to his workshop, got a ladder, and took the antenna up on the roof. All of the kids were outside watching him when he almost fell off the roof. Now I realized he was in no shape to hook up our new television and he might even blow it up. Mother had always told us that Daddy's calling wasn't to be an electrician. I ran into the kitchen and told Mother that Daddy was drinking and had almost fallen off of the roof.

"Your daddy promised me he wouldn't touch a drop today," she said. "Are you sure? I didn't see him drinking."

"I can swear to it, Mother. I just saw him throw an empty bottle under the house."

"Lord, let me get M.L. from next door to come and put that antenna up. He's an electrician at Sea Island, and he knows what he's doing. You go back out there and tell your daddy to get down off that roof!"

I was so excited; I couldn't wait to get our television working. We didn't have to ask the neighbors if we could watch their TV anymore. Now I could watch Mickey Mouse at my house.

Chapter 6

SOUTH CAROLINA, 1954–1955

The Mill

One day my father came home from work and announced that we would be moving to Aiken, South Carolina. The US Department of Energy was building a huge plant called the Savannah River Site that would employ nine to ten thousand people, and it covered thousands of acres. Daddy said it was a top secret project and we were not to tell anyone in the neighborhood or school about it. Something was said about the A-bomb. Daddy was very serious, and Mother seemed concerned and apprehensive. We all sat there dumbfounded. Why did we have to go with him? We didn't want to be incinerated by a nuclear bomb. Within days Mother had us busy packing our things; any foreboding feelings we had about top secret weapons changed to excitement about the move.

Daddy was unable to find a house in Aiken, but he soon found one in Fairfax, where he rented a small, white-framed house outside of town on a dirt road. It was one of several identical houses built by the owner of a sawmill close to the mill itself. The owner had made a wise investment, for the influx of workers to the area created a great need for rental housing. My mother said that it wasn't much bigger than a shotgun house. She was just kidding. Although it was long and narrow and sat very close to our neighbors, it did have very nice porches that looked out onto reasonably sized yards. Mother enrolled us in school, but it was only a few weeks before we were out for the summer and could play with some of the neighborhood kids.

One day Mother needed to go shopping for things for our new house. Since we only had one car, she took Daddy to work. We all piled into the car, eager to see what a top secret atomic plant looked like. We drove for miles and miles, passing through small towns that had been evacuated due to their proximity to the plant. The buildings and houses were still there, but all the people and signs of activity were gone. These were nothing but eerie, silent ghost towns.

Eventually we started seeing barbed wire fences and men with guns patrolling alongside them. When we arrived at the entrance gate, cars were lined up, and we had to wait. A guard came over and checked our car inside and out before he let us pass through. Nobody smiled at us. They looked at us more like we might be the enemy. It was very scary.

We drove into the compound and pulled up at a large building, where Daddy said, "You can let me out here." We watched Daddy merge into a crowd of hundreds of workers, and his head, the last thing I saw of him, quickly disappeared. Mother turned the car around, and as she drove up to the gate, the guards put us through a second inspection.

"Mother, what are they doing? Why do they have to search our car?"

"They're making more bombs like the one they used to blow up Japan," she explained. "The bombs are needed to protect our country, and the guards are making sure no one is carrying anything in or out that might be a danger to others. Your father is doing something very important for the government."

"Wow," we responded.

Vera and W.A. started talking about the bombs and what they did to the people in Japan. W.A. said he'd seen photographs of people whose limbs had been blown off and others who were terribly deformed by burns. "Ugh, that sounds disgusting," Vera said.

Mother said, "Y'all shut up. Stop talking about this. That was a horrible thing that happened during the war." For once we all did what she asked, and the ride home was mostly silent. It wasn't a very pleasant trip.

Daddy had given us fair warning not to go near the sawmill or the dump. Well, that was the first thing we did when we got home! W.A. and I decided to check out the sawmill. We walked out of the back door down a dirt pathway and through a little gate toward the mill. Giant stacks of lumber were curing in the hot sun, and the smell of freshly cut timber was wonderful. We spotted a huge rattlesnake crawling from one stack of lumber to another. I'm sure he was trying to find a cool place to sleep. We soon came to a road where trucks were driving back and forth delivering logs to the mill. We continued walking, and as we passed a house that was no more than a shack, an old, one-armed man ran out. He must have been the watchman. He yelled at us, "Get the hell out of here, or I will tell your mother!" That was a laugh. How about our father? Now that would get our attention.

We stopped and went back a little way until the old man was out of sight. Then we found a new route around him. He wasn't going to stop us. We made our way to the place where loud machine noises were ripping up the air with screaming metal and hammering blasts. We just had to see what was causing it. At last, there it was, a large engine puffing away with belts and pulleys, turning a huge saw blade that sliced logs like they were butter. Sawdust flew into the air as milled boards shot into a pile on the ground. A team of men grabbed the boards and stacked them onto a truck. It was fast action all round. Maybe Daddy was right about this place being dangerous.

I remembered a movie with a big saw in it like this one. The bad guys were going to slice the damsel in half, but she was saved just in time by Sergeant Preston of the Yukon. I looked at W.A., and he looked at me. The realization hit us at the same time. Our faces paled, white as mother's clean washed sheets. That old watchman—he must have lost his arm to this saw! We could almost see the spray of blood and bone when the saw ripped through him. Yuck! Oh no! We bolted out of there and went straight home. Our curiosity had been totally satisfied. Not one of us had any desire to go back there again.

Cucumber Babies

A farmer who lived down the road had planted a field of cucumbers. I was shocked at how fast they grew. It wasn't long before some black pickers came and harvested the cucumbers, leaving only the ones that had grown too large for market. Those unharvested cucumbers grew larger and larger until they weighed two or three pounds. The farmer told the people in our neighborhood that if we wished, we could have any cucumbers that were left in the field.

The little girl who lived next door and I took her little Red Rider wagon and walked to the field. We loaded it with as many cucumbers as we could pull. We brought them to my house, where we pretended to open a hospital for babies. Well, they were no longer cucumbers—they were our babies. Baby cukes. Some were girls, and some were boys. We took a nail and scratched eyes, noses, and mouths on them. We made little beds of pine straw, and Mother gave us scraps of cloth to wrap them in. We pretended that they were crying, and we rushed around, attending to the needs of each and every one. It wasn't long before our babies started rotting, some turning a yucky yellow green. W.A. came by and heard us crying over our babies.

"What's wrong with you two?"

"Our cuke babies are turning rotten. Look at their faces."

"Well, whaddaya expect? It's that stuff where Daddy works—it's in the air, and when you get exposed to radiation, it starts killing you. Besides, they're not cucumbers. They're aliens."

"They're not! There's no such thing."

I ran into the house telling Mother what W.A. said.

"Mama, he said our babies were aliens dropped off by a UFO and not cucumbers."

W.A. had seen the movie *The War of The Worlds*, and he was convinced he had seen spacecraft from another world flying around our house at night. I think it was airplanes patrolling the skies around the plant, but he chose to believe in aliens.

"Pay no attention to your brother. He doesn't know what he's talking about, and he'd better quit upsetting you girls."

We grieved like they were real babies when our cucumbers rotted, one by one. Mother told us this was just part of being a nurse. "Don't be sad. Even Florence Nightingale lost a patient or two."

We asked, "Florence who?"

Mother sighed. "Don't worry about it; you were good little nurses and did your best."

Little Rebecca

I heard the dinner bell ring at the sawmill letting the men know that it was time for lunch. I headed out toward the mill thinking that if they had all gone to lunch, no one would know if I was there. I walked down the narrow path in back of the house that led to the mill and to the roughly built shanty-type house with a tin roof. It looked as if it had been made of scraps from the mill. A rusty old fence encircled it, and it had a wobbly gate at the front. Inside the yard an old lady was sweeping. There wasn't a blade of grass to be seen. Her broom was made of small sticks tied together with strips of automobile tire tubes. A little girl was seated on the ground nearby, playing in the soil with a spoon.

I approached the fence and asked the old lady if that was her little girl. She abruptly stated, "No!" She said it so harshly that I must have jumped. She then said it was her granddaughter.

I asked, "What's her name?"

"Rebecca," she answered, and then she started asking me all sorts of questions, such as who I was and so on.

Suddenly the screen door opened, and an old man in dirty overalls stood in the doorway. It was the one-armed man who had chased W.A. and me away. He growled at the old lady, "Where is my lunch?" She threw her broom down and went into the house. I stayed and watched the little girl digging. I wasn't sure what to make of seeing that one-armed man again. Suddenly the little girl came over to where I was standing and stood looking at me. I just looked back at her. She was a beautiful little girl.

"Hi, Rebecca," I said. I put my hand through the fence, reaching for her hand. To my surprise she put her little hand into mine. I held it, drawing her nearer and nearer to me, just like Eliza used to do with me. Her eyes were so receptive, but she wouldn't say anything. Suddenly the screen door opened again, and there stood the man with one arm. "Rebecca, get in here!" She quickly turned and went into the house.

I ran straight home to tell my mother what I had seen. "Mama, Mama! There is a little girl who lives in that old shack. Her name is Rebecca."

The next day I went to the old shack again, and sure enough, the little girl was digging in the dirt. I bravely opened the gate and went into the yard. I continued to visit her for days until one day she wasn't outside. I went up to the house and gently knocked on the screen door. I didn't know what to call the old lady, so I called out, "Granny, Granny!" Getting no response, I called, "Rebecca, are you here?" There was no answer. This went on for several days. Finally one day, the old granny came to the door. She spit out her greeting as if talking to a salesman trying to sell her something overpriced and broken.

"What do you want?"

"I want to see Rebecca."

"Rebecca!" she yelled. Then suddenly Rebecca appeared at the door, and I asked her granny if she could come outside and play.

"Sure, you can have her. Take her and get her out of my hair. She's just like her mother—more trouble than she's worth."

I looked with dismay thinking to myself *oh, Mother gave me to Betty so maybe she does mean it*. "Would you really give her to me?" I asked.

"Yes. I'm sick," she said, "so why don't you take her?"

I was thrilled. I grabbed Rebecca's little hand, and off we went up the trail to my house. I walked proudly through the door, holding the hand of my own little girl.

"Mother, this is Rebecca; her granny said that I could have her."

Mother laughed. "She didn't really give you that child, did she?"

"Yes," I said with conviction. "She did. You just go ask her."

My mother wasn't about to believe that story. Later Mother came into the room where we were playing.

"You were right. She did give you that little girl. I just talked to the granny, and she told me she's unable to take care of the child now. She said would we take care of her until she feels better."

Mother insisted that we give Rebecca a bath and said this was the filthiest child she had ever seen. We filled the tub with warm water. From Rebecca's reaction, I'm not sure she had ever had a tub bath. Her hair was so matted my mother had to put Vaseline in it and gently comb out the tangles. It took lots of shampoo to get her hair and scalp clean. Mother put one of my shirts on her, and it hung long enough for it to be a dress. Then she pinned a pair of my panties on her. Mother promised to buy her some clothes next time we went to town.

Rebecca was so sweet, always holding on to my hand or leg. I thought it was wonderful to have my very own little girl. She stayed at our house for several weeks. My mother made repeated trips to check on the granny and to take her food. Then on one of her trips, Mother explained that the granny wanted Rebecca to come home.

I was in total shock. I turned and ran into my room, crying. Mother took the little girl back to her granny and wouldn't let me go over there for a few days until I calmed down. Several days had gone by before she thought it would be all right for me to visit my little girl. I followed the path to the old gate, stepped onto the porch, knocked on the screen door, and called to Rebecca. She didn't answer.

"Rebecca," I called again and again. No answer. Then I called out, "Granny! Graaaanny!" I could just make out the old woman's silhouette in the darkened room. Slowly she got up, hobbled to the door, and opened it.

"Where is Rebecca?" I asked.

"She's gone away," Rebecca's granny said. "She isn't coming back." My heart stopped. "The welfare people took her," she explained. "They are finding her a new home." My eyes filled up with tears, and try as I might, I couldn't say anything. She then turned away from me, and the door slammed shut.

I ran home to my mother. I cried so hard I thought I would die. Mother explained many things about life to me that day. She told me that I was feeling love for this child and—not only that—empathy too. I was putting myself in someone else's shoes. Poor Rebecca didn't have a family like I did. Our family might have been fractured, but it wasn't broken.

The Dump

The second site on the list of forbidden places to play was the dump. W.A. and I tried to convince Vera to go to the dump with us, but she didn't want any part of our shenanigans. One day, W. A. and I sneaked out of the house and crept down the dusty road, which made its way through a field to this mysterious place. As we got closer to the site, we got occasional whiffs of a foul odor. Being downwind, the odor just about knocked us over the closer we got.

"Hold your noses," W.A. suggested. "And find a stick to defend yourself in case we see any wild dogs." There were hills, valleys, and mountains of trash everywhere we looked. We took our sticks and started rummaging around in the trash. I found a large box with several ladies' hats inside. They were like new. I chose my favorites and stacked them, one on top of another, on my head.

Suddenly, W.A. yelled, "Hey, come see this!" I thought it might be a dead person, a dead animal, or just something gross. The closer I walked toward the heap where W.A. was digging, the stronger the odor became. I thought I would puke. W.A. had discovered a huge pile of rotten eggs that the local hatchery had dumped.

"Carol, listen—can you hear something peeping?"

Sure enough I could hear little peeps coming from within the pile of eggshells. We took our sticks and started scratching around in yellow slime. Suddenly a little chick appeared. These chicks were alive!

"Hey, find us a box," my brother ordered.

We rescued one little chick after another. Soon we had a couple of small boxes full of chicks. "Come on, let's get them home quick," W.A. said.

I could hardly keep the stack of hats on my head as I trotted down the road beside my brother. With two boxes in hand, every time my cranial tower tilted, I had to slow down, wiggle my head and neck about, and get things lined up again.

"What are you doing?" W.A. asked. He didn't understand priorities.

When the tipping hats got too far out of control, I'd yell, "Wait, W.A. I gotta fix my hats!" He'd scowl and shake his head, but he'd wait while I put the chick boxes down, got things adjusted, and then hustled on again. We couldn't wait for Mother to see our surprise.

The moment I stepped into the house with this stack of hats perched on my head, Mother started laughing, but it was short-lived when we showed her what we had in our boxes. Well, needless to say, she wasn't happy. She had a look that we called the evil eye, and if looks could have killed, we would have been dead. We had totally forgotten about the dump being off-limits.

"Don't you kids know that rotten eggs have enough bacteria in them to kill you and a city of a million people?"

Our eyes bulged out. "What? Kill you? Really?"

"What are you going to do with those chicks?"

"We don't know, but we had to save them from dying," W.A. said. "I guess we'll raise them."

"You'll have to talk to your father about that when he gets home."

It was only minutes before Daddy's car pulled into the yard. We ran out to tell him about finding our chicks at the dump.

"The dump! I should beat your butts for going there."

"Can we keep them?"

He shook his head and scratched his chin, saying, "Well…well." You could see he was wondering which was worse—our playing where he'd told us not to go or these baby chicks making pitiful peeps. W.A. and I held our breaths in anticipation of his verdict.

"We'll keep them."

"Yay!" we yelled and started jumping up and down.

We were not able to save all of the chicks. Soon we noticed that these chicks were different. Mother warned us that she thought that they were going to be goofy-looking chickens. Some had funny feet; others had a variety of physical abnormalities. We thought they were very cute.

Mother helped us care for our chick nursery, and later, Daddy built us a coop and pen. Now we were chicken farmers. We fed and watered our chickens every day. It wasn't exactly a freak show, but let's just say Mother was right. They were interesting-looking chickens. They were also tame from us picking them up and petting them. One particularly sad chick had a club foot and a weird little face. This became my favorite.

Daddy suggested that I go into the lumberyard at the end closest to our house and turn over some of the boards. I might find some bugs for this particular little chicken. The boards didn't just have a bug or two—they were loaded with termites. I'd carry my chick down there, turn over the rotten boards, and let her eat to her heart's desire. She'd go nuts trying to gobble them up. It made me laugh. Daddy said, "That chicken looks like a crow on a June bug." I decided to name this chicken Termite.

Sawdust Pile

Daddy started drinking again. He was on a binge. On about the fifth or sixth day, screams came from our room. Daddy was taking Vera's clothes, throwing them in the bathtub, and running hot water on them. Mother ran to stop him. He started fighting with her. He was in a crazed rage like a person possessed, rambling obscenities. He began striking Mother about the face and yelling at Vera. W.A. and I rushed into the room to see what was going on.

"I'll kill you and this little bitch!"

Vera was in total shock. Daddy had never called her an awful name like that before.

Mother screamed, "You kids run and hide. He's gone crazy!" Mother held him back as we ran for our lives out the front door, around to the back of the house, and toward the sawmill. Vera thought we'd have lots of places to hide there behind the stacks of lumber. We could hear yelling coming from the house and then gunshots. We didn't know if Daddy had killed Mother or not.

A short time went by, and then we could hear Daddy ranting and raving again, shooting off his gun, and calling for us to come home. Vera said she was afraid he would find us. We darted in and out through the stacks of lumber, making it all the way to the back of the mill to a mountain of sawdust. We climbed high onto the pile, slipping and sliding all the way. We started digging holes to bury ourselves.

"Take off your shirt and wrap it around your head," Vera said. "I'll cover you up just enough so Daddy can't see you and you can still breathe."

It wasn't long before we got very hot, sticky, itchy, and anxious to get out. We didn't say a word and only listened for a long time. Vera whispered, "I hear him! Shhh…he's out there!" We could hear him tramping around, uttering more obscenities. I thought my heart was going to explode.

We stayed hidden for a long time. Then we heard nothing. We waited and strained our ears to listen harder. The fear of being found overtook us.

Finally Vera said, "I'll take a peek." Every flake or chip of sawdust that she disturbed, no matter if it pushed an inch sideways or rolled a few feet down the hill, seemed too loud for comfort. After a long pause, Vera said, "He's gone. Let's go home."

We clawed our way out and scrambled down from the sawdust pile, brushing our bodies off as best we could. The sawdust stuck to our sweat-drenched skin, as much from fear as from the heat. We were itching all over as we crept back to the house.

What were we going to find when we got home? What might Daddy have done this time? It was too awful to think about, so we just kept moving forward and concentrated on being as quiet as possible.

"Look, Carol," Vera whispered. "I can see Mother through the window!" Vera tapped twice on the glass pane, and Mother motioned for us to come in. We slipped through the back door and into the kitchen like little mice.

"Where is Daddy?"

"He is passed out on the couch." Mother put her arms around us, crying. "Look at you poor children. Where have you been?"

"We hid in a sawdust pile," Vera answered. W.A. and I stood there speechless.

"Good God," Mother replied. "I've been out there looking for you everywhere. I was so afraid I'd lost you. What more can my poor children go through?" She wiped the tears from her face and gathered herself up. "Let's get you cleaned up." Mother assured us that Daddy would not be a problem.

"You children go take a bath and get the sawdust off your skin. I'll make us some supper. Go on now; you'll be OK."

We did like she said and then ate our supper. That night I slept with Vera, and W.A. slept in my bed to be close by if suddenly there was another problem with Daddy. We were so mentally and physically exhausted that as soon as Vera wrapped her arms tight around me, we both fell asleep.

The next day it was like nothing had happened. Not a word was said. We were all in a state of numbness. Daddy lost his job. He had not shown up for work that whole week.

We were soon packing to go back to St. Simons. It was a long, sad trip back to the island. We were tightly packed in the new Buick that Daddy could no longer pay for, and every few miles, I would feel tears welling up, and then I'd cry.

"Now why are you crying?" Mother asked in exasperation after the third round of grief. I told her I was sad to leave Termite. I knew the neighbors, whose care she'd been left in, would not keep their promise. I had said to them, "You must not eat her," but the way they looked at her told me she'd soon be chopped into pieces, dipped in batter, and fried. I was still grieving over Rebecca, too, and leaving my new friends. It was a combination of things that all seemed to have gone wrong. Most of all, I was deeply hurt inside by what had just happed with Daddy. The enchanted country life had come to an end.

Chapter 7

MY BIG BROTHER

My brother lied. He cheated. He stole! Sounds like a country song. Willis Alvin Hamby Jr. was only ever good on Easter and Christmas. He looked so stupid when he was all cleaned up. Mother would make him a new shirt and buy him new jeans, shoes, and a belt. He'd get his hair cut, and Mother would slick it down. Thank God this only happened on holidays. Daddy would tease him and say, "Grace, put a ribbon in his hair, and he'll look just like a girl." It infuriated W.A.

W.A. and I had a love-hate relationship. No one else could be mean to me but him; if anyone tried it, he would threaten to beat them up. My greatest protector was my mother. "Mama, W.A. looked at me. W.A. touched me. W.A. spit on me." She'd come running and give him the evil eye. "Leave her alone!"

I wasn't perfect—far from it. I was a tease. But he was my buddy. He included me in many of his adventures. I was one of the boys, and for that I was grateful, since I didn't have many girlfriends.

My brother and I would sit at the kitchen table playing poker with matchsticks in place of money. He was slick as a riverboat cardsharp with cards up his sleeve, down his shirt, or under his leg on the seat. W.A. had 101 ways of distracting me, too.

Every poker game ended the same. "Mother, W.A.'s cheating!" She'd come running and, after an inspection, would confirm he was guilty and that I was telling the truth.

"Pick a game your brother can't cheat at. Why don't you play slapjack?" Well, they misnamed that game. They should have just called it slapcarol. W.A. would hit my hand so fast and so hard the table and chairs shook. Even though my hand became blood red from his blows, I never gave in. I didn't care if my hand bled and fell off; I would do anything to be with my brother. We made such a huge ruckus Mother usually ended the card game by pointing to the door. "Out! Get out of this house and go play somewhere else!"

Mother said that W.A. was the greatest purse snatcher. She usually hid her purse in her bedroom. If she heard the slightest rumble in there, she'd yell out and accuse W.A. of looking for money. He was a super sleuth with a nose like a bloodhound.

Mother would buy little cakes called moon pies for Daddy's lunch box. She'd try to hide them, but with W.A.'s great nose, he could find them every time. Like a sly fox, he would slip into the kitchen cabinet, find her stash, and take only one, thinking she wouldn't notice any missing. Well, stupid, she bought one for every day of the work week, and when she came up short, she suspected W.A. of course. His pleas would ring out all over the house.

"Mother, why are you blaming me? Why don't you ever blame Vera or Carol?" She always told us thievery was a hanging offense, but she'd let him get away with murder.

You could always see the love in Mother's eyes when she looked at W.A. "My only son," she would say, and her tears welled up at the mere sight of him. But there were other times her tears formed for different reasons, like the time one of his teachers brought him home from school for fighting or when they'd want to have a big talk about his grades. I think her special bond with W.A. started when Daddy began verbally abusing him. Daddy would be sitting in his chair, drunk again, and saying things like "You mama's boy. Sissy girl. Good-for-nothing. You little bastard."

Mother could see the pain on W.A.'s face, but she was helpless to protect him. W.A. was determined to not let the tears that were welling up under his eyelids spill over and roll down his face. It was moments like this when we knew that Daddy had crossed the line. Daddy crushed W.A.'s spirit and scarred him in a way that would never heal. Everyone felt sorry for W.A., but like a scolded dog, he crawled back to his master each time, looking for Daddy's love and approval.

It was around 1956 that the county engineers cut a swath through the woods in back of our house with the intention of draining our yards during the rainy season. This ditch was ten feet deep and fifteen feet wide and ran the length of Broadway (about six blocks). The giant excavator had piled the sand into huge mounds, making the cavernous trench seem even deeper. Mother was always afraid that we would get some waterborne disease like swamp fever because everyone's septic tank would overflow during this time. My mother, being a nurse, always stressed not to play in this dirty water.

"This is a serious situation; it could make you very sick. I'm not joking around about it." Being children, we paid little attention.

Once the ditch began to fill with water, the frogs moved in. Soon there were plenty of them, and we loved to catch them. Where there are frogs, there are bound to be snakes feeding on them, so we were constantly looking out for snakes. We didn't have anywhere to put the frogs when we caught them, so we decided to dig tunnels into the side of the ditch. We dug as far as our little arms would reach. Then, we'd catch the frogs and put them into one of the tunnels. We'd place bars at the tunnel entrance using small sticks and hold them captive. Before long, we'd have a number of these tunnels making our frog jail. Of course, they'd all be released on good behavior.

Another favorite sport was to climb up and down the mounds of sand and then jump or slide into the ditch. Long grapevines hung from the overhanging tree branches in some areas. W.A. took Daddy's machete and chopped even more vines so that all of the kids had vines to swing on. These made a perfect spot for playing Tarzan and Jane of the jungle. My brother could swing higher than anyone else and would yell like Tarzan and then drop into the sandy ditch, landing on his feet.

W.A. was torn between being Tarzan or Audie Murphy, the great war hero who later became a movie star. Murphy was one of the most decorated soldiers in World War II.

W.A. and Ed (Boom) Hummel would sit for hours in the woods under the oak trees with their .22-caliber rifles. They called squirrels by making a kind of barking sound and waited for them to pop their heads up so that they could take a shot. Daddy always stressed that if you killed it, you had to eat it. Mother would boil the squirrels and then make a tasty gruel of cornmeal seasoned with butter and pepper.

These were not the only boys in the neighborhood who were out hunting squirrels. I could never understand how twelve- and thirteen-year-old boys could be allowed to have guns. They were such idiots! It was a wonder someone didn't get killed, since all of the little girls used those woods as their playhouse.

Daddy let all of us shoot, including some of the neighborhood kids. We sharpened our shooting skills when he pinned cardboard targets with clothespins onto the clothesline. If you were lucky and shot the target just right, it would spin around. Once, W.A. accidentally shot the clothesline wire in two. Mother just went nuts. Daddy told Mother to calm down.

"Grace, you never know when there might be another war and these kids will need to know how to shoot." That statement made her go even crazier.

Even though the war was over, W.A. was still on the lookout for spies who had not been told that the war was over. He was constantly taking potshots in the woods at imaginary Germans and Japs. When Mother heard the shots in the woods, she'd grab her heart and say, "Oh Lord!"

W.A. was a big fan of Davy Crockett, an American frontiersman and folk hero who died at the Alamo and whose story had been turned into movies and a television series. His deerskin clothes and coonskin cap with the striped tail had become icons and were the rage with all the young boys. One day, W.A. decided to try to make his own raccoon caps, thinking his would be better than the ones in the stores because those were fakes. He'd make them, sell them to the neighborhood kids, and make lots of money. It took several coon-hunting trips before W.A. had the perfect skins to make his caps. W.A. got upset when his first attempt at stretching the skins on the outside wall of the shop left them vulnerable to flies and they were soon full of maggots. With his next skins, W.A. was more successful. Mother was willing to sew them into caps, but he changed his mind. The skins smelled just awful, and they were stiff as a board. The neighborhood kids asked him, "Where are all of those coonskin caps, and where is all of that money you were going to make?" That really pissed him off.

Chapter 8

THE BACKYARD

Our backyard was like a three-ring circus, and Daddy was the ringmaster. When you walked out the back door of our house, you were shielded from the hot Georgia sun by a canopy of giant oak trees with long, twisting thick limbs. One large limb in particular hung across the path to the shop. This limb was the favorite sunning spot of an enormous, five-foot oak snake. Mother gave him a most appropriate name: Mr. Bishop, after our lawyer.

Daddy's work shed, a small building made from thick planks of oak, was always referred to as The Shop. As soon as you entered, mice, chameleons, or blue-tailed skinks would scamper into the corners or under the floor, a cool, shady area where a number of these critters made their home. There was one large blue-tailed skink that Mother called the Governor. She'd ask, "Has anyone seen the Governor today?" Mother had another friend, a green tree frog that lived in our bathroom. He was named Eugene, after our senator. Mother just loved politics, and she loved Eugene!

The shop was filled to the brim with every tool known to man. Daddy knew where every tool was located, and you couldn't even breathe on them without him knowing you'd been there. He'd go mad if one was missing!

Outside, to the left of the shop, was a junk heap of metal and car parts, boat trailers, and motors—all works in progress. There was also an area where Mother's washing machine and tubs sat.

Daddy was an excellent mechanic and welder. He worked on automobiles and other types of engines and did welding repairs for people. If you were caught standing nearby, you would be asked to assist him and become his grease monkey. He'd say, "Carol, bring me…" and then would come the long list of things to get for him. Standing on a five-gallon gas can, I'd rest my stomach on the car fender, bend over, and watch my father work.

"Daddy, what's this? What does that do?" He'd explain what he was doing and teach me about the parts of an engine and how it worked.

"You need to know about these things, because mechanics will take advantage of a woman."

Often when we were driving down the road, Daddy would ask, "Do you hear that ping?" I'd squint, purse my mouth, and listen with all the concentration I could muster.

"Yeah, I do."

"Can you hear that knocking?"

Again I'd say, "Yeah, I do." I could never rest in the car because I'd be thinking that the engine would blow up at any moment.

Daddy's little grease monkey seemed to get into a lot of trouble with Mother whenever she was messing around at the shop. One time Daddy asked me to look for a can of silver metal paint. I found it on a shelf covered with dust and spiderwebs. I took it to his long metal workbench, and he opened it. The contents looked like liquid silver.

"What kind of paint is that, Daddy?"

"It's specially made for painting motor parts."

I didn't have the vocabulary to describe its effect on me, but I was dazzled.

"It's really beautiful."

Daddy finished his project and then walked away. I picked up the brush and looked around for something I could paint. I looked down at my well-worn, scuffed flats and thought, "Why not?" I painted my shoes, and they looked good enough for Cinderella. A while later I wore them into the house to show Mother.

"Look at my shoes. Aren't they pretty?"

"Carol, those are your only shoes!"

"I know."

"Do you realize you have to wear them to school tomorrow?"

"Yeah."

She shook her head. "We can't buy you new ones until the next payday."

"OK." I'm not sure I understood what the problem was. I thought they were beautiful.

Well, I wore them the next day, and I was the laughingstock of the school. My shoes and I smelled strongly of that paint. I never gave up on my belief that they were beautiful though. I still loved them.

To the right side of the shop was where Daddy kept the dog pen, a large enclosure with a seven-foot-high wire fence, a gate, and four doghouses with canvas flaps for doors. These housed a number of different breeds of the highest-quality hunting dogs and coonhounds—redbones, black and tans, blue ticks, Julys, and walkers. Daddy would drive as far as Kentucky, Tennessee, or north Georgia to get a good hound.

When they got excited, a full concert of howls filled the neighborhood. There were few complaints from neighbors. I figured they were afraid Daddy would shoot them, for most of the neighbors would only yell, "Shut those fucking dogs up," and then quickly run back into their houses. But if the dogs or neighbors woke up Daddy, he'd be furious.

When Daddy was ready to go hunting, he'd open the dog pen, and the dogs would run around the house like just-released convicts. He'd yell, "Load up, boys!" and all of the dogs but Boo Boo would jump into the back of the truck. Boo Boo was too little and not tough enough to keep up with the big dogs, so she wasn't allowed to go. The dogs in the truck shook with excitement. Off we'd go with the chorus of howls trailing behind us.

We'd drive to Cannon's Point or Hampton. Dropping the tailgate of the truck, Daddy would say, "Get 'em!" With those words they'd yap, bark, and growl and go off in different directions. They'd dash through the palmettos and scrub bushes with their noses to the ground. Daddy would sit on the tailgate for a few minutes having a cigarette or two and wait for one of the dogs to hit a hot trail.

"Shhhhh…Listen. That's Sally. She's on a trail."

Sally was one of Daddy's favorite hounds. She was almost always the first to catch the scent of a coon. Daddy could recognize her voice from miles away.

"Listen—that's Sally. Nope, I think maybe Blue's found something."

Blue and Big Red were two of the toughest dogs. Determined and ruthless, they were often the last ones back to the truck. Daddy lost Blue in the woods many times because he was never ready to give up the hunt.

Then with excitement on my daddy's face, he said, "Nope, it's Sally! She's hot. That's my Sally."

Her barks would alert the other dogs, and they'd be in hot pursuit of a coon. Off we would dash then through the trails of scrub oaks and palmettos. I constantly feared getting left behind in the woods, and I had to work really hard to keep up with the men.

We'd locate the hounds at the base of a tree, jumping and barking with excitement. As the hunters shot into the tree, the frightened coon would drop to the ground. After a fierce battle between the coon and the dogs, sometimes the coon would be fast enough to escape, and sometimes he wouldn't. Daddy would hand me the coon by its tail and hang it over my back. Packing the dead coons was my job since I didn't have a gun to carry. Off the dogs would go again, and they would hunt until they reached the point of exhaustion. Daddy would start calling to them, yelling for them to get back to the truck. Loading everybody in, we'd head home.

The hounds were always hungry. We had a large bucket that we kept on the back porch where we'd put table scraps, if there were any. We'd heat a pot of water, add the scraps and several cups of Jim Dandy dog meal, and then give it a quick stir. This made a putrid brew that almost made you throw up. W.A. would carry the bucket down to the pen, and I'd follow. It took two of us to get inside the gate because the dogs were jumping on us, so excited to get their meal. We'd have to right the scattered old dishpans, and I would scoop their food into the pans while W.A. tried to make the dogs wait. Dogfights often broke out as I rushed around to each pan while W.A. kicked the dogs away. Then we'd each get a shovel and pick up all the dog poos in the pen. Yay! We were finished.

In a few days, we would help Daddy dip the dogs in a tick and flea solution. The woods were full of ticks that would attach themselves to the hounds' skin and could cause disease and inflict great pain. Daddy would take Mother's washtub, which pissed her off, and fill it with water and a foul-smelling solution. The dogs knew exactly what was about to happen, and they'd try to hide behind their doghouses. Going into the pen, we'd drag a dog out one at a time and take it to Daddy. Trying to get a dog into a washtub that it didn't want to get into was a funny sight. Legs were in, then out, and then back in again. Daddy wasn't a patient man. He'd quickly grab the dog around the middle, flip him, and thrust him deep into the water. With his legs flailing, the dog was dunked—a Baptist-style baptism. When he was released, he'd run, shake, and roll like he'd been born again and was overjoyed about it. They acted so funny running around the yard and would come back to give us unwanted kisses while we were busy baptizing the next dog. We'd all be soaked to the bone with solution. The hounds, the yard, and all of us smelled like that dip for days. Our hounds were like members of our family, and we did our very best to take care of them.

Daddy frowned on spoiling the hounds. They were for hunting and were not considered personal pets. But there was one exception—Boo Boo. A runt from one of the many litters, she just wasn't all there. Boo Boo was a black-and-tan hound and very small for her breed. Everyone loved her, especially Daddy. Often he would get drunk and sit on the front-porch steps hugging Boo Boo and saying, "Grace don't love me anymore, but you do, don't you?" Boo Boo would lick him in the face. He'd hug and kiss her and keep repeating, "Boo Boo, Grace don't love me anymore, but you do, don't you?"

"Bill," Mother would say, "get in this house! Everybody going up and down the street can see just how drunk you are." Ignoring her, he'd continue to sit there hugging Boo Boo.

Getting past Daddy and Boo Boo was always hilarious. Daddy would catch you and bite you. Then, Boo Boo would get excited and bite you too. The Russians had launched a satellite called Sputnik with a dog in the nose of the rocket. We wanted to volunteer Boo Boo for the next flight. Picking on Boo Boo wasn't allowed; after all, she was Daddy's drinking buddy and confidante.

Daddy's Drinking

Located along Frederica Road were four bars: Golden Isles Club, Wayside Grill, The Oasis, and Pete's Place. Pete's was my daddy's favorite watering hole. Many times my mother would ask me to go look in the bars to find Daddy and ask him to come home. I would walk along the long, sandy back road to Frederica Road. I'd enter the first bar feeling sheepish and praying my daddy was there. I'd walk around and look through the smoky haze, trying to locate my father. If he wasn't there, I'd go on to the next bar and then the next. Most of the time, he was at Pete's. The Oasis catered mostly to golfers.

Once I found him, I would walk over and say, "Mother wants you to come home." Boy, that would piss him off. He'd give me a dirty look and order me out. I'd grab some peanuts from the dish on the bar and run like hell back home. I always ran as fast as I could in order to get home before he did. I'd be panting as I ran through the door and into the kitchen where Mother was sitting.

"He's coming. He's coming." Then I would disappear and hide before he got home. Daddy, being intoxicated, would stagger through the door and sit at the table looking down at the plate of food that my mother had so lovingly prepared. But the alcohol would have taken his appetite away. He would sit there for hours, propping his head up with his hands. All the steam was out of him. Mother would eventually guide him, stumbling and staggering, toward the bedroom. Often they only made it to Daddy's chair in the living room.

When Daddy passed out in his favorite chair—the throne—he sat like a slain giant. At times we thought he was dead, but he wasn't. The stench of stale liquor and cigarettes filled the room. There were periods when he didn't seem to breathe. He'd be in a state of total calm, and then he would suddenly gasp for another breath.

No one sat in Daddy's chair when he was in the room. The sound of his approaching footsteps pounding on the wooden floors was our cue to vacate it and quickly. The location of his chair in the middle of the living room, between the kitchen door and the living room door, could not have been worse. It left only two feet of space to get around him, and his reach was longer than that. There were two ways to exit. We either had to run like hell or tiptoe like little mice passing a sleeping cat. If by chance you were caught, there was hell to pay. In a flash he'd snare you and pull you to his lap, squeezing the daylights out of you.

My father had huge, fat teeth. They filled his mouth with abundance. Playfully biting and nibbling on your ears brought him some kind of pleasure. Yelling and screaming for help usually brought someone, most often Mother, to your rescue, securing your release with cries of "Bill, you're hurting Carol" or whomever he had captured. He just laughed it off. I found the way he smelled repulsive. Cigarettes, booze, fish, gasoline, oil, and body odor.

Eventually, something would have to be done with him. Mother would try to wake him up, pulling and tugging at him and asking him to please go to bed. When that didn't work, we children would try to wake him by tickling and shaking him. We'd say, "Daddy, you need to go to bed!" With great persistence and Mother's help, we'd finally make him get up, and guide him to the bedroom. She would lay him down on the bed, remove his shoes and socks, unbuckle his belt, and slide his pants off. Covering him up, she'd sneak out of the bedroom and close the door ever so quietly, just as if a baby were sleeping.

Mother prayed for some kind of peace. Hell no! From the bedroom my father's voice, slurred by drunkenness would cry out, "Grace, Grace, I want some pussy. I want some pussy!"

I could see the disgust on her face. She was so humiliated. She would jump up and run into the bedroom to try to quiet him.

"Bill, the children are just outside the door sitting in the living room! They can hear you!"

She'd go lie with him for just a couple of minutes. His hugs were so tight that she thought she would stop breathing. Then, he'd become weak as a kitten and release her. She'd slowly slip out of the bed and come out snickering, "Well, he's no Casanova." After this ordeal she'd sit at the kitchen table with her elbows planted on the red Formica table, hands under her chin supporting her head and a cup of coffee beside her. The kitchen light would beam down like the noonday sun while the window fan hummed, bringing in a breath of cool air. With no husband to lean on, her only companions would be the tear-jerking country songs played on the radio. She'd be totally worn-out.

If Mother was lucky, Daddy would be able to go to work the next day, and this wouldn't be repeated the next night. My father was a binge drinker. He wouldn't drink for days and sometimes weeks. We never knew exactly what would set him off on an episode, but once he started, he'd drink himself into oblivion. He would have blackouts leaving him with no memory of what he'd done or where he'd been. Often he would get locked up overnight for being intoxicated and passed out in a bar. Other times he would get into fights and be put in jail. He never became so dependent on alcohol that he had to have a drink to cope or survive on a daily basis. But a binge did something to his brain, and after a few days, he would become a madman.

Fearful of his actions, W.A. or Vera would grab me up and whisk me out of Daddy's reach. There were many times during his crazy, wild rages that we would climb into the attic space. Being the smallest, I needed help to get up there. All of us would hide in that scary, dark hole, and lying close together, we'd hear Mother fighting off the blows of our drunken father's mighty fists. She'd run from room to room screeching like a cornered cat. Other times we would climb out the bedroom window and run to the back of the house to hide behind the shop. We'd huddle arm in arm. Often, we would just have on our bedclothes. We never knew if we were shivering from the cold or from fear.

Sometimes Mother would come with us, but most of the time, she would stay with him, fearful that he would hurt himself or set the house on fire. When she did leave with us, Daddy would come out of the house with a gun, shoot into the sky, and yell obscenities. I was constantly afraid that he would severely hurt her or one of us. We would stay huddled together until he passed out. Mother would quietly tiptoe inside the house just to make sure he wasn't playing possum, which he did on occasion. Shivering from the cold, we'd climb into bed wondering what could happen next. After an ordeal such as this, falling asleep was difficult, but when you finally did, it was like you'd fallen into a deep coma.

Each time we suffered one of these episodes, Mother would pack the car, intent on leaving Daddy. We'd scurry around, packing our favorite toys and clothes in brown paper grocery bags until the car was spilling over with us and our things. As we sat in the car waiting for Mother, I would pray that she would just get in and drive away. But Daddy would start begging and pleading with Mother not take his children away from him. Sure enough, she'd give in to him. I so wanted to go and live with my Granny Mathis. We'd finally pile out of the car in disgust that Mother had changed her mind about leaving him. I'd go into my bedroom and throw my things across the room. This was an ongoing pattern in our lives that repeated with increasing frequency.

I often thought of Mother as being weak for her decision not to leave Daddy. I later realized that it took strength for her to walk back into what was certain hell. The next day she would look numb and in shock, as though she were feeling nothing and thinking nothing and just suffering total fatigue. Daddy would start begging and crying, promising to change. In a few weeks or months, he would start drinking all over again. She was trapped. Or maybe Daddy was the one who was trapped. Well, we children were for sure. When you get older, you can see things a little differently, but I still feel sad that she didn't have a better life. Our mother certainly deserved better. She was degraded past anything you could imagine. But she still loved him and stood by her man.

Love is patient; love is kind; love is not envious or boastful or arrogant or rude. It does not insist on its own way; it is not irritable or resentful; it does not rejoice in wrongdoing, but rejoices in the truth. It bears all things, believes all things, hopes all things, endures all things.
1 Corinthians 13:4

Chapter 9

ST. SIMONS ELEMENTARY SCHOOL, 1950–1956

Carol

We all loved going to school. Daddy usually woke up at about five o'clock in the morning to make his breakfast and lunch. Then he would set an alarm for us for the appropriate time and go to work. When the alarm went off, we would all stumble out of bed and try to eat the leftovers on the stove. Trust me—it's hard to warm up cold grits. Mother would often make oatmeal and cinnamon toast. Our clothes were always starched and ironed to perfection. Mother would say, "Smile," and we'd each give her a big toothy smile and get a quick inspection of our teeth. She would give us a kiss and then take quarters out of her little black change purse pressing one into the palm of every child's hand.

"Don't lose it."

Out the front door we'd rush, down to the sidewalk and to the street. Walking down Broadway we'd join up with the neighborhood kids at Demere Road. The oldest kids would stop us from crossing the road until it was clear. As we stood on the side of the road, lots of teasing would commence. When the bus arrived, we would line up in a disorderly manner and climb on the bus. Going south on Demere, we would pick up the Palmers', the McCaskills', the Stephens', and the Grays' kids and then turn left onto the East Beach Causeway to Ocean Boulevard. Just a couple of miles on the right, we'd come to St. Simons Elementary School, which was built of red bricks with floor-to-ceiling windows. The school first opened in September of 1944. The school bus would pull up to the front of the building and drop off the elementary school children. Then, the bus would proceed to Brunswick, where the high school children were dropped off at Glynn Academy, the fifth-oldest school in the United States and where Betty went to school.

The school was located only one block from the beach, so often our teachers would let us have our recess there. The kids loved it. The children would cross Ocean Boulevard and go down the beaten sandy path to the beach. There we would take our shoes off. Boys would race back and forth, darting in and out of the water chasing shorebirds. The girls waded in only ankle-deep and jumped as each new wave rolled in, leaving sea-foam on the wet sand. Often dogs that belonged to Chuck, one of the boys at school, would come and play with us. The cool water was such a relief from the stuffiness of our shoes. I wore saddle oxfords to school, most of the time with socks. I even wore sandals with socks. Mother didn't want the dirt to touch our feet because you could get all kinds of diseases. This was the accepted fashion on St. Simons. After half an hour of beach play, the teacher would blow her whistle and collect all the children. Back we would march to our classrooms carrying the few shells and sand dollars we had found and placed safely in our little pockets.

St. Simons Elementary was a great school. I wasn't very smart com-
pared to most of the kids. I was extremely shy. It was in the fifth grade
that my teacher, while doing a twenty-twenty eye chart examination,
discovered that I couldn't see very well. The teacher taped a cardboard
chart up on the blackboard. She examined all of the children, but when
she got to me, I failed miserably. In order to see the smallest letters, my
nose practically had to touch the chart. How could I have gotten to fifth
grade when I could barely see the writing on the blackboard? My teacher
must have thought I was retarded. A note went home telling my mother that I had to have a professional examination. Mother rushed me to
Brunswick to see the optometrist for an eye exam. They were all shocked
at how poor my eyesight was. The frames of my new glasses were a beautiful shade of blue, but the lenses were bifocals. On my first day back at
school, the kids all laughed at me and said I was wearing granny glasses.
My teacher didn't help by telling the class Benjamin Franklin invented
bifocal lenses. It made me feel just awful. My glasses were so strong that
at first it made me nauseous. When I walked I looked like a toy soldier
marching because I hadn't learned to look through them properly. The
color and clarity of everything was almost too much to take in. I could
see for miles. The trees were amazing with all those leaves and branches.
I could see now. What a miracle!

Apart from having to wear glasses, I had other health-related concerns
because I fed off of my mother's hysteria. One day at school, our teacher
told us about rickets. Rickets was a disease that sailors got from being on
ships for months and not eating fruits and vegetables. Poor children also
got it from bad nutrition. She showed the class a picture of children with
rickets. Their little legs were all bowed. I thought, "Oh my God. I'm poor,
and sometimes I go to bed hungry." I could just see my playmates, Katie,
Delores, Brenda, and me, with our little, bowed, wobbly legs, trying to
hold one another up.

My reaction was to make an all-out assault on the icebox. I was so full
of fear that I wouldn't be able to eat enough to fight off this terrible disease.
I drank the PET evaporated milk right from the can when Mother and
Daddy were not looking. I'd wipe off my lip prints from the top of the can.
Mother thought she was going crazy. She would open a new can, and I
would sneakily drink half of it. She couldn't believe that it was half-empty

after just opening it. Giving the can a Dick Tracy examination, she would shake her head and give me that look.

I started eating mustard sandwiches too. I had heard they were good for you, and I believed it because Granny Mathis had us take mustard baths and would make mustard plaster poultices when we were sick. It had to be true! I even went to war with W.A. for the last piece of chicken or biscuit at dinner. "Oh Lord," I thought, "please don't let me or my friends get rickets!"

One day our teacher sent a health notice home to our parents about the symptoms of polio. The school already had one case. This message just flipped my mother out. It read,

---

Message to Parents
Watch for Early Signs of Sickness
Polio starts in different ways—with headache, sore throat, upset stomach, or fever. Persons coming down with polio may also feel nervous, cross, or dizzy. They may have trouble in swallowing or breathing. Often there is a stiff neck and back.
Act Quickly—Call Your Doctor at Once!

My mother panicked every time one of us sneezed or acted funny. How could anyone know if anything was a symptom of polio or just the normal childhood sniffles?

The teacher gave us a card from the March of Dimes with slots that you could put dimes into to help raise money for polio research. I would ask Mother and Daddy every few days if they had any dimes. You had several weeks to fill up the card. During those weeks—I hate to say it—I would take a dime or two to buy candy at Mr. Brooks's grocery store. I knew it was wrong, but if Mother didn't give me money, I would borrow it from the March of Dimes card. Mother would ask, "Isn't your card full yet? It should be full by now." I don't think I ever filled up that card completely, and I have no idea how much money I owe the March of Dimes.

I can remember the excitement at school the day we lined up to get our little cup with a sugar cube in it. The nurse put several drops of vaccine on it, and I popped it into my mouth. What a relief! A cure for polio. All that money I had sent to March of Dimes must have helped. Now it was one thing I wasn't going to die from or be crippled by, like the little girl on the poster who had to walk with crutches. And I wouldn't have to live in an iron lung.

The bus ride home from school was always exciting. As the kids piled off the bus, the first thing we did was run over to where a row of rusty mailboxes stood. Vines grew all over them. Each box had a possible surprise inside. Who would be the lucky kid today? No, the surprise wasn't a letter from Roy Rogers or Dale Evans. It was something much more exciting. It was a snake! These were green snakes.

"Green snakes won't bite you," W.A. always said, but they could sure scare the hell out of you. I always thought that a bigger poisonous snake like a cobra or some other exotic species like the ones you saw in the movies might make our mailboxes its home. Of course we didn't have these kinds of snakes on the island. Hearing a loud yell, you would know who the lucky person was that day. Everyone would laugh hysterically.

When someone found a snake in his or her mailbox, W.A. would quickly rush over and catch it. He liked to scare all of the girls with it. If Eliza was working at the house that day, he'd take it home to scare her too. Our mother hated snakes more than anything. W.A. would try to scare her too. Watching girls or women go into panic over snakes was one of his favorite forms of entertainment, and he never got bored with scaring everyone with them.

After school, I would play until suppertime, and then I'd help wash the dishes. I didn't study at home, and no one pushed it. After all of that playing, I was too tired to do homework. I don't know how I managed to never fail a grade.

Chapter 10

DDT, Water, the Swamp, and Vinegar Relatives

There were several things that brought me pure joy. One was running behind the fogging machine. You never knew when it was coming, but you could always hear at least one kid yelling about its arrival. It made a sound like no other. I can still call up the sights, sounds, and feelings of pleasure—running in and out of dense fog, kids yelling, and my mother screaming, "Get away from that machine! You might get run over—a car driver can't see you in that fog. And it's not good to breathe that stuff." The stuff was DDT. It had a lovely clean smell that I liked.

The second-best thing was the smell of our water: rotten eggs. The community artesian well must have hit a sulfur mine. Our relatives would come for visits during the summer months, and they hated the smell and taste of our water. Making tea or Kool-Aid with it didn't help improve the taste. Holding your nose while drinking didn't either.

Thank God for bad water and the bugs, or our relatives would have been there all the time. They always took my bed, and that really pissed me off. It meant I had to sleep on a floor pallet along with all the roach bugs. Yes, lots of roaches. I couldn't sleep at night for the fear that a roach bug would crawl inside my nose or my ears.

Our relatives' most favorite activity was going to the beach. Unfortunately, it only took a couple of days before they had horrible sunburns. They would have to be doused with vinegar to ease the pain. We'd then have to come up with an alternative plan for entertainment. The Okefenokee Swamp near Waycross was plan B for sunburned visitors. Everyone knew this was where Pogo Possum lived with all of his funny friends. W.A. and I loved Pogo Possum comic books. Vera would read them to me, giving each of the animal characters a funny voice. It made us laugh.

We'd hire a boat and a guide who would paddle us into the swamp to see all of the water plants. One type of plant actually ate bugs. Our guide told stories about the Indians and the prison escapees who once hid in the swamp. He called it the Land of the Trembling Earth. The water was so black—it reflected your image as in a mirror. The alligators were huge, especially Old Roy. He was the biggest and oldest in the swamp. I was already familiar with alligators and took the sight of them in stride (after all I was an alligator hunter), but my relatives got a real thrill out of seeing these prehistoric-looking reptiles.

They always had a snake display at the swamp park as well. It was exciting to see the snake handler come out with his boxes, and the sounds that emanated from the boxes indicated there were definitely snakes inside. We were amazed that he would take them out of the boxes and handle them. After that exhibition we would head back to the island, and our mothers were glad to leave, especially after being creeped out by the snakes.

Ruins of Fort Frederica, St. Simons Island, Ga.

Now another day was spent at the beach. After the picnic, swimming and romping on the beach, we returned home. Our mothers soothed our little sunburned bodies with vinegar baths.

The next day, it was off to Fort Frederica so that our little bodies could recover from the previous day's sunburns. We would visit the museum and climb on the ruins of the fort, sit on the cannons, and pretend to shoot the Spaniards as they came up the river. Seeing what we thought was a log suddenly turn and go in a different direction to the tide was a source of great excitement. It was no log. It was a monster-size alligator! The boys loved it—they went nuts and shot the gator with imaginary cannonballs.

My aunt Nadine took about a dozen bricks from the fort ruins to put in her new house that she was building in Marietta. Her principles weren't the highest. Mother tried to discourage her, but she paid no attention. Aunt Nadine actually made each of the kids carry a couple of bricks back to the car. Mother was not happy! I felt like a thief. Mother said, "You all *are* thieves!"

After Fort Frederica we'd stop at Christ Church, the site where John and Charles Wesley preached to the colonists from Fort Frederica under the oak trees. Even then I knew this was sacred ground. You felt it the moment you stepped foot on the brick pathway that led to the beautiful white church with its stained-glass windows. Christ Church was built in 1820, but during the Civil War, it was almost destroyed. It wasn't until 1884 that Anson Dodge Jr. financed the construction of this new church.

The grounds were always especially beautiful when the dogwoods and azaleas were in bloom in the spring. The huge oak trees were covered in Spanish moss, which hung like torn lace drapes and whiffled in the breeze, adding to the ghostly, mystical atmosphere. The cemetery provided a history of the people who once lived on the island. Reading the headstones, we'd learn about their lives, babies who died at birth, people who lived to be a hundred, and soldiers who gave their lives in war. Camellia bushes would drop red, pink, and pure white, rose-like blossoms, which we'd gather and put on the graves. It was a somber place, but most certainly our favorite.

After leaving the church, we would stop by the Sea Island Stables and arrange for a ride on the mule train. The mule train was a series of attached bench seats on wheels pulled by a driver in a Jeep. The ride was completely open-air, and you had to hold on tight to avoid falling out. The driver would take us to Sea Island and let us see how the rich people lived, for this island was inhabited exclusively by mansions and money. There were oohs and aahs from everyone. The driver then took us back past the fort and Christ Church and made a quick stop at the First African Baptist Church, built in 1869 by former slaves who lived on the island. Finally we returned to the stables.

After what seemed like a month-long visit, the relatives would leave. Mother discussed adding more bedrooms to our house with Daddy, but he said if he did that, we'd have relatives visiting us all the time. The best thing about having relatives stay with us was that their visits made my mother happy. I liked it because we ate better when they came, but I was also happy to see them leave. They would leave smelling like pickles; their bodies had been wiped down with vinegar so many times to treat their sunburns that Daddy said they were starting to stink.

Chapter 11

BILL HENDRIX AND THE
ISLAND ART CENTER—1952

I credit my love for art to Bill Hendrix, who became my mentor at a very early age. The first time I met him, I was engaged in stealing his fruit, though it didn't seem like theft to me. All the kids in the neighborhood liked to climb the mulberry tree in front of the house on First Avenue. Every spring that sixty-foot tree would be near to bursting with sweet red berries.

I had no fear of heights and would climb to the top, where the sweetest, juiciest berries were plentiful and ripe. And the day I met Bill Hendrix, that was where I was, eating mulberries. A voice called to me.

"Little girl, please come down before you fall. And please don't eat those berries. They have worms in them."

The man whose voice interrupted my feast and brought me down the tree waited until I reached the ground.

"My daddy says the worms won't kill you."

He laughed. Oh, this man was handsome. He looked like a movie star!

"What is your name?"

"It's Carol." I was surprised he didn't scold me for being in his yard.

"My name is Bill," he replied. "Where do you live?"

"Over there." I pointed through the woods in the direction of my house.

"Oh." He paused for a second and asked, "Do you babysit?"

"Yes."

"Well, my wife Mittie and I have a baby boy. His name is Carey. I would like to talk to your mother about you sitting for us."

"OK!" I was so excited that I ran home skipping and singing one of my favorite little songs. "Here we go round the mulberry bush, the mulberry bush…"

It was only a few days before I received a call to babysit. Mother cleaned me up and sent me over to the Hendrixes' house at the appropriate time. Walking into their house was like entering a movie set. They had beautiful furniture and, best of all, a grand piano. Wow! I was so impressed.

A tall lady with dark hair came out of the bedroom holding a baby. He was so cute. She spoke sharply to me, asking questions and giving me orders. It was too much for me, and I almost panicked until I remembered what Mother had said just before I left home. "Don't forget—I'm just around the corner if you need help." I wanted to make a good impression. After all, it was my first babysitting job. Making my own spending money would be wonderful. As Bill handed me the baby, he patted me on the head, reassuring me that I would be just fine.

After taking care of their baby for several weeks, I happened to ask Bill where he worked. My eyes flew open when he said he was an artist and had a studio at the airport. Oh no! *Only a few weeks earlier my brother and I had broken into a decrepit, deserted building at that very airport.* I just felt awful. What would he think of me if he knew?

W.A. and I had been wandering around the old abandoned radar training center at the airport and forced a door open to snoop inside. We walked down the long hallway and peeked into each room. One of the rooms had been turned into an artist's studio. We walked inside and found tables with tubes of paint, brushes, and pastel chalk. Large drawings of nude women—showing breasts, belly buttons, fannies, and all—were hanging on the walls. What a shock! Our giggles and laughter rang out and nearly gave us away, but nobody heard us. The place seemed deserted that day. As we looked around, we didn't disturb anything. We knew that our daddy would have killed us if we did. I never told Bill about this incident. I was too ashamed. After babysitting for several months I became very attached to Carey. Even Mittie began to seem friendlier toward me.

I was so sad when I heard the Hendrix family was moving away. But Bill said he wasn't going very far and that I could come visit him anytime at his studio. He was building something called the Island Art Center, a place where all artists could come and paint.

During the summer, on my way to the gas station to buy Cokes and candy, I checked on the construction of Bill's studio. Of course, I was always hoping that I would see Bill there. Even though he was very busy most of the time, he always greeted me with kind words and asked me how my art was going.

In 1952 the art center was completed. On one of my visits, Bill asked me if I would model for him.

"Just come over here and sit on this stool. I want you to model for my painting class." He posed me and asked me to sit real still. I sat like a statue and almost forgot to breathe; I wanted to please him so much. I must have done a good job, because I continued to model for him and his classes. I'd come back to the studio as often as I could just to be with the other artists hoping that Bill would need me to help him with something. Often, I would sweep the floors, clean brushes, and scrub the sinks. As a reward, he would give me short art lessons and let me observe his classes. The art center gave me a place to go when I felt lost and lonely, and the experiences there were enriching my life.

Chapter 12

My Wandering Years

Lighthouse, St. Simons Island near Brunswick, Ga.

*W*hen I was about twelve, I would go to The Pier by myself. By hook or by crook, I would get there. I might ride with a neighbor, steal W.A.'s bike, or just walk. My journey to The Pier would take me south along Old Demere Road, across Ocean Boulevard, and right onto Beachview Drive.

Once you got to Beachview, you couldn't miss the lighthouse. Built in 1872, the white tower was over a hundred feet high, with a two-story red-brick keeper's cottage with white-painted, wood-framed windows; a porch; and railings. It was a beautiful sight. The original lighthouse, built in 1810, was only seventy-five feet high. During the Civil War, the Confederate soldiers dynamited the lighthouse and keeper's cottage in order to prevent the Yankees from using it as a navigational aid.

I loved climbing the iron spiral staircase with its 129 steps that took you to the top of the tower. Exiting the staircase through a door, you stood on a three-foot-wide balcony that wrapped around a rotating glass lens in the center. Inside the lens was a light that reflected for miles, keeping ships and boats safe and on course. A waist-high railing surrounded the balcony and prevented falls. You got a bird's-eye view of the ocean with its shrimp boats, and you could see Jekyll Island and Cumberland Island and for miles around. One day the wind almost blew me off.

Vera told me that the lighthouse and the cottage were haunted, so I would take a peek in the rooms of the keeper's cottage to see if I could catch a glimpse of the ghost of the keeper, Frederick Osborne. He was killed in a duel by the assistant keeper, John Stephens, for saying something about Stephens's wife. Whatever Osborne said, it must have been awful nasty.

From there I'd wander over to Neptune Park, which had been named in honor of Neptune Small, a slave and faithful servant of the King family at Retreat Plantation. Neptune was the childhood playmate of their son, Lord. He brought the body of Lord back to St. Simons after he was killed in the Civil War, and then Neptune returned to the war to serve Cuyler, their youngest son. Neptune stayed with him until the war ended. The site of the park was land originally given to Neptune Small as a reward for his service.

Inside the park was the Casino (no, not a gambling place), a huge, two-story, multi-complex building with big letters on the front: *CASINO*. I'm sure gamblers from out of town were shocked when they went inside and found it full of kids and without a gambling table or slot machine in sight.

Through the front door, you'd walk into an area on the right where a long refreshment bar sold drinks, hamburgers, hot dogs, and fries. On the other end was a huge open dance floor with a jukebox and, along the sides, small tables with chairs. The entire area stood open to the air by means of windows as big as garage doors. Teenagers loved to sit in the windowsills. Most of the time, it was a hangout for the older kids.

"Little kids not welcome! Get lost," the older teenage boys would shout.

Located just behind the concession area was an Olympic-size swimming pool with diving boards. To get inside the pool, you would have to take a short flight of stairs down to the pool level. An attendant would take your money (twenty-five cents), and you would be directed to go through the footbath. My daddy said it was the same solution that they used on the farm for cattle with foot-and-mouth disease. I do know it was strong! It would eat the skin off your feet. W.A. told me that they didn't have a footbath at Sea Island's pool. I thought that was a little strange. "Don't they get foot-and-mouth disease over there?" I wondered.

I loved swimming and jumping off the high diving board. When the big boys or the swim club would come, I would have to leave the deep end of the pool so that they could practice. We loved to watch Jimmy Bankston dive. He was an amazing diver, and when he competed in the swimming races, nobody could beat him.

The next part of the Casino was the bowling alley. It was upstairs and adjacent to the swimming pool. W.A. worked there setting pins. It was hot and muggy and a hard job to do; you had to move fast, and when the place was full, you never got a chance to catch your breath, let alone take a break. W.A. later got an easier job working at a gas station.

Two flights of stairs brought you up to the second floor, my favorite part of the Casino. This was a skating rink with the same big windows as on the main floor, and when they were open, the breeze would cool you off as you skated and looked out at the ocean. We skated around and around to all kinds of music, from waltzes to rock and roll. Daddy wouldn't let us wear the little, short skating skirts, but he did let us wear shorts and longer skirts. Vera's favorite was a pink skirt with a black poodle on it. We had a wonderful time skating at night. The lighthouse beacon would flash outside, the stars would twinkle in the night sky, and the ocean breeze would cool your face.

A balcony surrounded the rink, so you could go out there and look at the ocean on one side or look down to the swimming pool on the other. I pretended that I saw Esther Williams, the famous movie star known for her aqua musicals that featured synchronized swimmers. She was very beautiful and a favorite with the young girls. The little girls I played with in the pool pretended to be her. We could only stay underwater a few minutes before coming up gasping for air. We couldn't understand how she could stay underwater so long! I think that the joke was on us: no one could stay underwater that long. After all, it *was* the movies.

After the Casino I'd walk across the U-shaped drive and up a sidewalk to the theater to look at the poster displayed for the coming attraction. Then, stepping down into the open-air atrium at the center of the building, I'd do a few dance moves, spinning like Ginger Rogers. The library on the other end of the building didn't interest me at all. I wasn't about to waste my summer reading. Instead I'd skip down the stairs to the swings and monkey bars for just a minute. I'd swing or hang upside down and watch the people eating at the picnic tables under the massive oak trees.

My next stop would be the Ferris wheel and merry-go-round, where I would see if I could get a free ride on the wheel. I would stand there for ages gazing at the wheel until the attendant felt sorry for me.

"You want a ride?" Mr. Curtis Stevens, the owner of the amusement rides, knew I was not a tourist but a local kid. Roger, the kid he hired to attend to the rides, would try to make me sick by keeping the Ferris wheel going and going and not letting me off. Or he'd scare me by stopping the wheel and leaving me sitting at the highest position on the top. He'd grab a rag and pretend to work on the motor and then make a motion or yell that it was broken. There was also a little train with a brightly colored engine pulling ten or more cars that encircled the area, but I wasn't interested in that ride. It was for little kids. I think it was a toy for Curtis. He was often seen playing the engineer, just riding round and around by himself. I wondered how many miles he drove that train to get to where he already was.

Next, I'd check out The Pier. My father and his friends always sat on the bench at the entrance to The Pier. They were the old guard, talking and gossiping about everyone and everything. Their eyes would roll at the sight of the pretty girls, and there would be the occasional wink. I remember once one old guy had his foot up on the bench. I noticed something strange hanging from underneath his swimsuit. It was the grossest thing that I had ever seen. I had never seen male private parts before, not even my brother's or my father's. And I didn't think that I wanted to see any more. I told Vera about it, and she said that they were balls. They didn't look like balls to me.

The Pier was quite long, with benches running its length toward the sea, and a canopy roof over the main walkway kept the sun off of you. The end section that ran parallel to the shore didn't have a roof, benches, or railings, so you could easily fall off if you weren't careful. This was where shrimp boats or sailing boats could tie up and dock. Lots of people fished off of The Pier. You had to be careful and watch their casting rods, or you might get hooked. It was fun to ask each fisherman, "Have you had any luck today?" They'd proudly display their catch or comment on the ones that got away. The crabbers, using wire baskets with chicken parts tied on, occasionally let a blue crab escape. Screams would ring out as the crab, with its pinchers snapping at people's toes, tried to find a place to escape back into the ocean.

I loved it on the Fourth of July when a number of navy ships would tie up at the end of The Pier, one after another. They let us come on board and tour the ships. They gave us cookies and lemonade. I thought the sailors were so handsome. Even at twelve, a man in uniform thrilled me.

A quick stroll took me up Mallery by Trade Winds Cafe, Palmer's five-and ten-cent store, the bank, the community market, Roberta's, Ward's Drug Store, Strother's Hardware, and the icehouse. I would stop at the icehouse and check to see if there were any broken pieces left where they dispensed the ice, and I'd find one to suck on, quench my thirst, and help cool myself off. During the summer Mother bought big blocks of ice for when she made homemade ice cream. They had ice even in the plantation days. Ships brought it down from the North. That must have been a rare treat for those people.

Finally I'd head home by Queen's Court motel, go up Kings Way, and turn right on Frederica, which ran parallel to the airport strip. Mother and Daddy said the airport strip was a dangerous road. Mother always reminded us to look out because the golfers either had too much to drink at Sea Island Golf Club or were rushing to the Oasis for cocktails. Most everyone used this road to blow out his or her car engine. Often the cops were sitting off to the side of the road waiting for the speeders.

Stopping at the slave cabin where Eliza once lived, I'd gather a bouquet of bright pink, purple, and white phlox for my mother. I'd proceed right at Demere and turn left onto Broadway. Slowly dragging myself home, I'd step onto the porch and walk through the living room and into the kitchen, where I'd find Mother. I'd proudly present to her the beautiful bouquet of phlox. Smiling, she'd give me a big hug. I would be exhausted and starving, so I'd sit at the table, and Mother would give me something to eat and drink.

"What have you been doing all day?"

Knowing all the time that I wasn't supposed to venture so far away from home by myself, I'd give her a sweet, innocent look and say, "Oh, nothin', Mother."

Chapter 13

POLK SALAD

Oh, the joys of the rites of spring! The island was its prettiest at this time of year. The azaleas, dogwoods, and oleanders were in full bloom. The evergreen oaks had pushed off their brown leaves for bright green, and birds were seen and heard everywhere in great numbers. My favorite was the red cardinal. The brown thrasher was our state bird. I never understood why we had a state bird that was so ugly.

Every spring Mother asked me to help her pick a mess of polk salad. It grew wild in the back woods. With our brown paper grocery bags in hand, we walked out the back door past Daddy's shop and deep into the woods.

"Pick only the young green leaves and not the large stemmed ones," Mother said. "And don't you dare eat any of those red berries. They are poisonous. You'll see birds eating them, but they are not for people."

Granny Mathis swore by polk salad. It was known to purify your blood. She was part Cherokee Indian, and she said that the Indians ate it. It would keep you from being infected if you were bitten by mosquitoes, ticks, fleas, chiggers, or gnats. I thought those were very good reasons to eat polk (poke) salad.

After filling our bags to the brim, we walked home, careful with every step to look for snakes, sandspurs, and stinging nettle. Stinging nettle had a pretty white bloom that would trick you into picking it. Every part of it caused you tremendous pain if you touched it. Mother knew how to make tea from it. It wasn't a favorite of mine. I did like sassafras tea, but only if it had lots of sugar in it. It tasted like root beer. These teas also purified your blood.

After surviving the wilds of the mission into the back woods, we arrived at the back porch and stepped quickly into the kitchen before the screen door hit us on our butts. Mother emptied our bags of polk salad into the sink, submerging them in water to remove the bugs. Stinkbugs were the worst kind. If you touched them, they smelled to high heaven, and you didn't want to ever eat one. Mother didn't concern herself with most of the other hitchhikers. "If you eat a bug, it won't kill you."

Now, as if making a witch's brew, Mother put the big kettle on the stove. She put the greens into a large pot and covered them with the boiling water. She brought that water to a boil again and then drained the greens into a colander. This was done three times. The kitchen filled with steam. She also filled a small pot with water to make tea. I always feared she'd make nettle tea, and I imagined that stinging, prickly stuff going down my throat, even though she only made her nettle tea from the root.

After Mother thoroughly drained the polk, she chopped the greens and placed them in a bowl with cream and beaten eggs. She scrambled the eggs and polk in bacon fat and served them up with corn bread and regular sweet tea. Thank goodness.

As she dished the polk salad onto the plates, Mother said, "You'll love this. It tastes like spinach."

I didn't like the taste of polk salad or spinach. Popeye could eat my share anytime. I'm sure he would have loved both. It pleased my mother though, knowing my blood was going to be pure for another year, and if it made her happy, it made me happy.

Chapter 14

OUR NEIGHBORS

The Prentices

Jamie and Mildred Prentice had four children: Barbara, Jimmy, Linda, and Johnny. Mr. Prentice was a full-time housepainter and also ran the projector in the Casino Theater at The Pier. The projection booth didn't have air-conditioning, so it was extremely hot! Both jobs were demanding. He painted all day, and then you'd see him day after day, week after week, arrive home to change clothes and, minutes later, rush out the door to get to the theater so he could start the movie on time. When Jamie Prentice wasn't busy working, Mildred had him remodeling the house. She just wasn't satisfied with anything for long.

Unfortunately for them, they had to be our neighbors. Even I wouldn't have wanted us for neighbors. Mother made sure that our lawn was cut and tidy and that our gardens were well kept. But once you got past the patio in the backyard to Daddy's domain, it was awful. There was a huge, smelly dog pen full of hounds that howled or barked at the slightest movement in the yard or woods. Hell broke out every time they saw a cat. Junk lay scattered all over the place. Sounds of welding machines running, hammering, and clanging on metal became the neighborhood music. Rowdy men drank while they cleaned their fish and butchered hogs. Daddy would take the fish and hog guts into the woods behind the shop and bury them. Later, animals would dig them up, and the guts would be strewn all over the place. Daddy scared every neighbor within blocks around us during his wild, crazy binges when he shot guns off and yelled. No one dared to confront him because of his reputation for fighting. Daddy had been locked up several times by the police for fighting. He carried a huge pocketknife with him all of the time. He used it mostly like a sportsman would, but he would pull it out in a flash in an unsportsmanlike manner. During one fight he got a big cut on his nose. Boilermakers had a reputation of being bad, and that's what my daddy was—a boilermaker. He did everything he could to live up to the reputation.

Our yard was separated from the Prentice property by a page wire fence. Whenever Johnny was outside, I'd walk through Mother's azaleas and stand by the fence, and Johnny would always come over and talk. I would have given anything if he could have come over and played with me. He could have had so much fun with us, going fishing and hunting, working on cars, and playing in the woods. His father didn't have much time for him because of his work schedule. If his mother saw us talking, she would yell, "John Marvin Prentice, you get in this house!" He'd run quick as a flash inside. She acted like she and her family were too good to associate with us. I didn't think it was fair for her to treat me that way, and I couldn't understand why she didn't like me. I was just a little kid. They went to the Baptist church as we did, but I guess God's second-greatest commandment didn't pertain to them.

You shall love your neighbor as yourself.
Mark 12:31

The Glissons

Neighborhood boys

Maybe God took pity on me for the humiliation I suffered on the Prentice side of the house, for on the other side, M.L. and Mary Glisson lived with their three children, Wayne, Delores, and Brenda. Mr. Glisson worked in maintenance on Sea Island at the Cloister Hotel. One of his jobs was to run the movie projector at night for the guests. On Sundays most people had checked out, so he could invite his kids and a guest (me) to watch the movie. Before starting the film, Mr. Glisson would go to the kitchen and bring back a special treat, a bag of yeast buns and pastries. I had never eaten fancy buns with seeds on them—only biscuits and loaf bread. These pastries were unbelievably delicious.

We had to sit quietly so as not to disturb anyone. Once we got to listen to a famous violinist practicing a type of music I had never heard before. My parents certainly never listened to classical music; they were country music fans. I was amazed by the beautiful music that came from that violinist's instrument.

Well, did this place ever impress me with its beautiful furniture, drapes, and carpets. There were waiters and waitresses running around serving all the needs of the guests. Movie stars, presidents, and other famous people stayed there. So this was how the rich lived! I was catching on to what class distinction was. They were rich, and we were poor. I couldn't see anything in between. Even pretending to put myself into that lifestyle would have been just too big of a dream.

The Coulsons

Sara Jane, John and Carol

Jack and Ruth Coulson had three children: Sara Jane, John, and George. They lived on First Avenue. Jack was from Bebside, England.

Sara Jane, one of my favorite little friends, was so sweet and kind. We loved playing with dolls. One time a relative of hers who lived in England sent her a Queen Elizabeth coronation doll when the queen was crowned in 1952. This was the most beautiful doll I had ever seen; if I could have only had a doll like that, I would have loved it to bits.

I talked Sara Jane out of some perfume that she had one time. The bottle was labeled *Evening in Paris Eau de Toilette*. I convinced her it was made from water taken from a toilet with some sweet smell added into the bottle. I took it home and then felt real bad because I had done the wrong thing. I never enjoyed using it, but Vera certainly did.

Sara Jane, her brother John, and I used to go over to the airport. We girls skated on the tennis courts, and John rode his little peddle car. When school was out for the summer, Glynn County Parks and Recreation hired a local teenage boy to give tennis lessons and manage the courts. That was short-lived. A few of us kids signed up for the lessons, but by July the only person to show up was that poor teenager. You'd see him sitting in the shade of a nearby building with a water soaked towel covering his head. That asphalt must have been two hundred degrees.

Seeking an indoor place where it was cooler, sometimes we'd go to the armory at the airport and watch the older kids play basketball or the girls take dancing lessons. The Coulsons' house was another place where I found refuge. Even though they didn't have a lot, they invited me to dinner many, many times. Mrs. Coulson was hard to get along with. She was very bossy and grouchy but had a heart of gold. Daddy said there was no way he could live with *that* woman. I wish Mother had been as strong as she was and maybe kicked Daddy's ass every once in a while.

I don't think Coulson (that's what Mother called Ruth) realized that she was probably Mother's best friend. She always defended Mother and helped her in any way she could.

The Hummels

Boom and W.A.

Red and Byrdia Hummel had two children: Jo Patsy and Ed (Boom). They lived on Demere Road. Red was a housepainter, and Mrs. Hummel was a quiet and very kind housewife. Jo Patsy was a pretty brunette, smart and very nice to me. When Vera got married, she was maid of honor. Jo Patsy married a sailor named Frank who was originally from Ohio and very handsome. Frank picked on me all the time to see just how mad he could make me. Many times I thought, "Buddy, you're getting close to being kicked in the balls," but I'd hold my temper and shrug my shoulders, saying to myself, "Oh, you have to forgive him; he's a Yankee." I'd have to remind myself that I was a lady. I had a huge crush on Boom, but he didn't know it. As far as he was concerned, it was like I didn't exist.

All of the Hummel family called me Tootie. This nickname was given to me by my mother when I was a small child. While she wasn't looking, I had climbed up on the table and ate most of a tutti-frutti cake that she had just baked. Boom also called me by my nickname, which I loved.

The Hummels made a big mistake in letting our family come over and watch TV. They couldn't get rid of us. Saturday nights, Daddy and Red watched the fights, but on Sunday nights we all enjoyed *The Jackie Gleason Show* and then *The Ed Sullivan Show*.

"Carol, it's getting dark outside," Daddy would say. "You need to come home with me." Daddy had the flashlight.

Sometimes I asked Mr. Hummel if I could stay and watch a little more TV. He always said yes. I would stay until they had to throw me out. There was a price to pay for staying late. I had to walk home alone through a long section of sandy road that was dense with vegetation. At night, it was a tunnel of darkness, and you couldn't see your hands in front of your face. I always dreaded this section. Imagining I was a gazelle, I'd run and leap through the dark until I made it to where the lights of the houses shone. Then I'd let out a deep sigh of relief as I reached my house to live another day.

The next morning I would have to walk back up that road to catch the school bus, so I'd check the tracks in the sand to see how many snakes and animals had crossed my footprints in the night. Chills went down my spine whenever I saw the slithering marks of a snake where my feet had been. Despite the fearsome critters in the dark and my having to walk that path alone, when the next Saturday and Sunday came around, I'd risk my life all over again for just two hours of television. I was a TV junkie, totally hooked on that screen.

The Petersons

Harry and Peggy Peterson lived on First Avenue with their two sons, Harry and Jamie, and their daughter, Gale. They were Yankees. Mr. Peterson was the manager of the Sea Island Golf Club. We kids just couldn't understand how you made a living working at a golf club; after all, our fathers had jobs where they worked as mechanics, welders, painters, electricians, and teachers.

The little girls in our neighborhood were very excited when we heard that Mrs. Peterson just had a baby girl. Katie, Delores, Brenda, and I wanted to see this baby, so we all marched up to the Petersons' house and knocked on the door. Mrs. Peterson opened the door and asked us with her very dignified manner why we were there.

"We heard that you had a baby girl, and we came to see her. What is her name?"

She smiled and said, "Gale," and we all commented that it was a pretty name.

"Ladies, just give me a moment, and I'll bring her out to meet you."

Katie, Carol, Delores and Brenda

We waited and waited. Suddenly, out rolled the biggest black baby carriage we had ever seen. It was the Cadillac of baby carriages. The chrome on the wheels glistened in the sun. We were bedazzled. My little blue baby carriage was nice but nothing like this one. I almost forgot about the baby for a second or two. The carriage was so high that poor little Brenda could hardly see inside of it. We all strained to get a look, and then, there she was…the Peterson baby. She was so beautiful! She was bald-headed with only little wisps of blond hair, and she had the brightest blue eyes I had ever seen. She peered around like a little bird, not knowing which of us to look at next. We were not allowed to touch her because our hands were dirty.

We thanked Mrs. Peterson and told her that her baby was beautiful. Walking back home, we agreed that the baby was very cute, but oh my God—*that baby carriage!* We talked about it for days and days to come.

The Brewers

Olin and Margie Brewer had three children: Gale, Billy, and Mark. Mrs. Brewer was a kindergarten teacher and Mr. Brewer a brick mason. They lived on the corner of Demere and Broadway, far enough away that our hounds and Daddy's craziness didn't affect them.

After school our gang would go down to the Brewers' to see if they would let us watch *The Mickey Mouse Club* on their TV. It didn't always happen, and we would be disappointed. Margie was very strict. You had to sit on the floor, and there was no clowning around allowed. She would let you go to the bathroom or to the kitchen to have a drink of water, but you couldn't do it too many times or she would scold you. When the program was over, you were excused to go home.

Once the gang decided we'd be peddlers. One peddler, who called on Mother and the other neighbors all the time, had really good things for the kitchen. He also sold candy and cookies, but Mother wouldn't buy much from him, saying his prices were too high. We took a large Red Rider wagon and went to our houses to collect things we thought we could sell to make some money. Mother gave me a small collection of things to sell, and the other kids brought things from their houses. Taking our wares, the gang went up and down Broadway, over to First Avenue, and then up to Frederica Road, knocking on doors and asking passersby if they wanted to purchase any of our wonderful goods. We soon found out that being peddlers was not as easy as we'd thought. We didn't sell many items at all. I knew then I wasn't cut out to be a peddler.

Several things were left over, one of which was a toaster the likes of which I'd never seen. Intrigued, I took it home and showed it to Mother.

She laughed, "I don't think that will work for our family."

This toaster had two sides that dropped open. You put one bread slice in each side and closed the doors. It would toast all right, but the slices went from white to burnt black in seconds. Disgusted with the burnt results, I agreed with Mother. When she made us toast, she'd fill a large pan with slices of loaf bread that had been spread with lots of butter and sprinkled with cinnamon and sugar. She broiled it until it caramelized. Mother's toast was so good it would melt in your mouth.

The next day, Mrs. Brewer was at our front door. She wanted her toaster back. Her kids had not been given permission to sell any of the items that they took. I hid behind my mother because I could see that Mrs. Brewer was very angry. Mother said she'd be happy to return it. She walked to the back porch and retrieved the toaster from the trash can. When Mother handed it back to Mrs. Brewer, she didn't mention where the toaster had spent the night. Margie Brewer thanked Mother, saying she was ever so happy to get this toaster back. Mother and I shared a little giggle. We couldn't believe they actually ate burnt toast. Maybe that was why the kids tried to sell it.

Not only did the peddler come to our house but also the insurance man called on us for payments once a month, as did the furniture man, Mr. Sweat. My father used to buy my mother the absolute ugliest furniture in the store, hoping to surprise her. It surprised her all right, but her reaction was usually shock, and then it turned into anger. She would be mad for days. Once he picked out this sofa and chair covered in bright-green plastic with metallic sparkles. My father thought they were the most beautiful things he had ever seen. That sofa didn't last very long. Someone (it is a mystery to this day who) sat down with a screwdriver or something sharp in his or her back pocket and poked a hole in the plastic. Then it ripped. Daddy taped it over and over, but it didn't hold. Mother tried to cover it with a blanket, but it would just slide off. When Mr. Sweat came to collect, she would have to scratch around in her purses and go through Daddy's dirty pants pockets trying to find enough money to make the payment. Mumbling and shaking her head, she'd say, "Paying for an ugly, torn sofa. How maddening!"

The Howards

W.A.

The Howards lived up the street just two doors away. Mr. Howard and Easter had five children: Joanie, Lily, Paul, Ruthie, and Katie, my very pretty and sweet friend. One day, all of the kids went together to see our first 3-D movie. It was called *Creature from the Black Lagoon*, and it was the scariest movie we'd ever seen.

We had our very own Black Lagoon on the other end of Broadway. It was the pond where all of the yards and ditches drained into. It had quite an odor, but we didn't mind. It was deep and so black you couldn't see the bottom. All of the kids would sneak off to have a swim there. One day while swimming, Katie let out a scream that sent chills down my spine. The shock on our faces was universal, for we all thought the same thing: that creature from the Black Lagoon has her! We swam over to rescue her, and while the tears ran down her face, we guided her to the bank. We were shocked to see so much blood coming from her foot. Her toe was almost cut off and was bleeding profusely.

"Please take me home!" Katie screamed.

With W.A. on one side and me on the other, we managed to get her home. Katie's mother was very upset over her injury and even more so when she learned we'd been in that nasty pond. Her mother said, "You could have drowned in that pond!"

Katie got a terrible infection, and we never went back to the Black Lagoon. We were convinced it was the creature that almost got Katie that day.

Mr. Howard worked at the Dixie Paint Factory. He was a quiet, kind man and a big baseball fan. Their TV was always tied up with him watching baseball games or shows about politics. On special occasions he would invite the neighborhood kids to a baseball game in Brunswick. We really enjoyed these games because most of us played some form of baseball or softball. We'd watch the Brunswick Pirates play. They were a farm team for the Pittsburgh Pirates.

Katie's mother, Easter, was a very sophisticated lady with prematurely white hair. I thought she was so beautiful and had excellent taste in clothes. Katie got her good looks from her mother. We enjoyed putting Pond's cold cream on our faces and playing with her mother's scarves and costume jewelry.

Easter also was a great cook. She made the best biscuits I had ever tasted. Her biscuits were big and round, thin, crunchy, and very brown. There must have been a pound of lard in each and every one of them. I would walk into her kitchen and ask her if she had any leftover biscuits. She usually did. I suspect she always made extra for me. She would say, "You look over there on the stove under that towel, and you'll find some." I would grab one or two in each hand and start munching.

"Mmmmm, Mrs. Howard, you make the best biscuits."

"Now, Carol."

"It's true."

Once Daddy caught me eating in our kitchen, and he asked, "What is that you're eating?"

"It's one of Mrs. Howard's biscuits. She makes the *best* biscuits!"

There was silence in the room. With Mother standing there, you'd think that I'd committed a cardinal sin. She looked so disappointed.

Daddy said, "Let me taste that biscuit."

I handed it over. He took a bite and paused.

"That is the worst biscuit that I've ever tasted. I wouldn't feed it to my dog."

I looked confused. Mother broke out in laughter. Never, ever tell a southern cook—especially your mother—that someone else's biscuits are better than hers! It is a cardinal sin.

Chapter 15

GATOR POND

W.A. was allowed to drive Daddy's old blue truck when he was only thirteen. Not only that—he could drive it most anywhere he wanted. Many times at dusk we would load up Daddy's aluminum boat and paddles and drive to the gator pond on the north end of the island. We'd unload the boat and slide it into the black water, looking around to see if there were any water moccasins. Shadows from the hanging Spanish moss on the oak trees made it feel a bit spooky at the water's edge, so we didn't hang about.

Out we paddled to the middle of the pond, where W.A. shone Daddy's large flashlight across the water surface, looking for the reflection in gator eyes. The greater the width between their eye reflections, the bigger they were in size. Grunting out gator calls, we'd try to coax them toward us. We'd splash the water with the paddles, trying to get their attention. Gators are very curious creatures. Soon, with their tails leaving rippled wakes on the water, they'd head toward our boat. W.A. always chose what he thought was the biggest one, aimed his rifle, and shot. There would be a big splash, and we'd look to see if he had killed a gator. After that he always said the same thing.

"I might have to jump in and wrestle this one; he's going to sink to the bottom of the pond." That was such a joke, because we were not even sure he had killed one. I don't think a .22 bullet is capable of killing a gator.

Usually the mosquitoes and gnats got so bad we'd have to go home. Upon our arrival, everyone wanted to know how many gators we had bagged and brought back with us.

"Sorry! We shot a bunch of them, but they all sank to the bottom of the pond. I wanted to dive in and retrieve them, but Carol wouldn't let me. She was too scared to be left in the boat on her own."

"W.A., you're lyin' again. You don't even know if your bullet scratched that gator. You probably missed by a mile." Then we'd both start laughing and telling more gator stories, but everyone knew they were just stories.

Chapter 16

DADDY KING FISHERMAN—LATE 1950S

my Daddy + fish

*D*addy was a king fisherman. He looked and acted like Humphrey Bogart and patrolled the rivers like he was on the *African Queen*. He knew his way through the creeks, rivers, sandbars, and mudflats. Other

fishermen would sit and wait for him to leave the marina so they could follow him to his favorite fishing holes. It pissed him off. He didn't want to
share his fishing spots with everyone. He loved the challenge of the sport,
and he was extremely good at it.

Daddy would clean the fish, wrap them in paper, and stack row
after row in our freezer. His bounty fed our family and many others in
need of a meal. Fresh fish was often delivered to Eliza and other friends.
Or we would hear knocks at the back door from people with the same
request.

"Mr. Coon Bill—he say I could have a fish or two." Onto the porch
they'd come and select a nice fat fish or two from the freezer, or if they
wanted, they could have another meat stored in there.

Daddy didn't always give fish away. He used it to barter when he
needed help in the yard. We'd often drive to the Crow's Roost, a place
off of Old Demere Road on the corner of Arnold Road, by the huge
oak tree. There you'd always find a number of black men sitting and
standing, waiting for day work. They must have had a system as to who
would be next because only one person would come over to the truck
window and ask, "What kind of work do you need today?" Daddy
would make a deal as to how much fish and how many dollars they'd
get. These men didn't know it, but Daddy hated yard work with a passion. I never saw him work in the yard—not once. The closest he ever
came to doing yard work was the time he picked up a stick, but it was
only to hit a dog. If those men had this information, they'd have made
a much better deal.

Daddy taught all of us children at an early age how to fish. He would
rig up an old rod and reel with a lead sinker tied to the end of the line
but no hook. We'd practice casting in the side yard for hours and hours.
Daddy had no patience with anyone who didn't know exactly what he
or she was doing. When he was out on the water fishing, he didn't have
time to fool with an amateur. If you got a backlash, you would have to
untangle it yourself. You could sit there for hours trying to untangle
the line, and Daddy would only help you if it was impossible to do.
When you got good enough with your casting and had some precision,
then you could go out in the boat fishing. Mother would join us on

occasion. She liked going out on the sandbar at Pelican Spit so that she could walk around while fishing instead of just sitting in the boat.

Mother always said, "If Daddy's fishing or hunting, he stays out of trouble." Well, that was far from the truth. It was just wishful thinking on her part.

Chapter 17

The Trouble with Coon Hunting

One evening while we were out coon hunting, Daddy lost one of his best hounds, Big Red. Daddy was determined to find him. We drove up and down the sandy roads at Cannon's Point, crisscrossing through the woods and yelling and hollering for Big Red. It was after midnight when we had to call it a night. Daddy said he'd come back later in the morning and try to find him. After all, it was a school night, and I needed to go to bed.

Getting up that morning and going to school wasn't easy. I was in a stupor as I left the house to catch the school bus. Stumbling into class I sat at my desk, laid my head down, and fell asleep. My teacher came over and shook me.

"Carol, wake up. Why are you sleeping?"

I proudly explained that I went coon hunting with my daddy, he lost Big Red, we couldn't find him, and…and…and…

"I thought so," she said. "You're sleepy, you stink, and you have marsh mud on your face and arm. I want you to stay after school and see me. Tell your brother that I will be taking you home after school." You see, we didn't have a telephone at that time.

Mother was shocked to see me standing on the porch with my teacher. She was used to W.A. being brought home from school but not me. She opened the screen door and asked my teacher to come in. They sat on the ugly green couch.

"Mrs. Hamby, you have to stop Carol from going coon hunting with her daddy. She is failing her schoolwork. She's tired and smells awful!"

"I know," said Mother.

I could tell she was upset, and it was more than frustration or worry. She was embarrassed by all this. It was bad enough when W.A. got in trouble, but boys are expected to get in trouble sometimes, or else they wouldn't be boys. When daughters get in trouble, it's a reflection on the mother.

"It's her father who thinks it's OK. I told him she shouldn't be going hunting."

"Well, it isn't OK. Do I need to speak with him?"

"No, that's not necessary," Mother said. "When I explain you've come all the way over here to express your concern about Carol sleeping in class, he'll listen."

An instant was all it took to end my coon hunting. It wasn't long before Daddy and the boys went coon hunting again. They left me at home, and I got very upset.

"I'll just go hunting on my own," I mumbled.

Looking at the guns propped up in every corner of the house, I picked up my brother's .22 rifle and stalked out the back door, heading for the woods behind the shop. A group of wild banny chickens were scratching under the trees for food, and in their midst stood a colorful rooster. I put my trusty rifle up to my cheek, took aim, and fired. Bang! I hit the poor chicken in the head, and blood started spewing as he flipped and flopped on the ground. I let out a scream and dropped the gun. I didn't know it was loaded.

Suddenly, I heard Mother yelling, "Oh my God! Oh my God! Carol, are you OK?" She ran up to me and grabbed me.

"Yeah, I'm OK. I didn't know the gun was loaded, Mama. What a stupid thing for W.A. to do, leaving this gun loaded!"

Mother looked at me with a fury in her eyes like I had never seen before.

"You could have killed yourself or shot someone else!"

In a flash her arm went back, and she walloped me. She marched me back to the house, spanking me all the way. When we got inside, she scolded, "Go get on your bed, and stay there until your father comes home!"

I was on trial that night. My parents explained the seriousness of my actions like they were prosecutors in the courtroom. And when they got past the part about endangering myself and others, they told me I was a little girl, not a boy, and they were concerned about me being such a tomboy, as if that, too, were a crime.

"You're going to become a lady and quit this foolishness, come hell or high water."

They tried me and found me guilty, and then they sentenced me.

"No coon hunting! No gator hunting! No guns! No jeans! That's final."

And it was.

Chapter 18

Bus Trip and Mama's Little Girl—1955

It was late in the summer of 1955 that Mother and I took a trip to Huntington, West Virginia, on a Greyhound bus to see Betty. It took almost two days through some of the most mountainous roads that I had ever been on. And boy, was I disappointed when I got there! They lived in the suburbs of a large city that was all concrete and asphalt with the houses close together and very few trees.

Betty was expecting her first child. By now she had been married almost five years. Betty's marriage got a little shaky during Kenny's two-year service in the navy. He married her when she was only sixteen and then left her with his family—people she didn't know. She grew homesick many times and wanted to come home. First, they didn't have the money, and second, he was afraid that if she ever left, she wouldn't come back.

I was totally bored and had absolutely nothing to do. Kenny's family was nice to us, but Mother and I couldn't wait to leave. We didn't care how awful the bus ride was; we just wanted to go home. I was actually happy to see my brother when I got home, but I wouldn't tell him.

The trip was good for Mother and me. It brought us much closer. I spent more time with her, and she showed me how to cook certain things and how to use the pedal sewing machine. She would let me sew little scraps and strips of fabric to practice using the machine and also to make doll clothes. Of course they were just terrible looking. Mother said that she liked them! She called them swaddling clothes.

Mother would not go to Brunswick very often. It seemed like the island held her captive. That trip across the causeway felt as if it were fifty miles long. The cost of gasoline was part of the issue, and not having a dependable car—or just not having any money to spend in the stores—was another incentive to stay put.

Shopping at Friedman's for shoes was fun. Mother always bought me ugly saddle oxfords. I hated them, but the jingle sold me on them. "I'm Buster Brown; I live in a shoe. That's my dog, Tige; he lives there too." The store also had a shoe-fitting fluoroscope machine where you could view your feet and see where the bones were in relation to your shoes. I didn't care if some said it was a gimmick or that it might give you radiation. Mother and I were confident that it helped me to get a good-fitting shoe. I probably only got a little radiation. I was starting to wonder just how much radiation it took to make you glow in the dark. I feared that I was getting close after all the exposure I received in South Carolina from the nuclear plant.

Downtown Brunswick had four beautiful parks with benches. Mother and I would stop by one and sit to rest. We'd always see people we knew and have a chat. Then we went off for more shopping. Mother and I would only look at the dresses at Altman's and O'Quinn's. They really had beautiful things, but Mother would go there only to get ideas for making our clothes. There was one exception for Mother. She did purchase her underwear and stockings there, plus that dreaded girdle that took two of us to help her into.

We would then go to Kress's department store to shop around for all kinds of miscellaneous things, like pots, bread pans, kitchen utensils, or fabric and thread. We'd have lunch, and then we'd head back home. On the way, we'd stop by the farmers' market and buy butter beans, butter peas, tomatoes, or peaches by the bushel that she could prepare and can for the winter months. If figs were in season, we would stop at Buck and Celia Buchanan's on Demere and purchase figs that they grew. Mother would always get into long conversations with Celia. They were a very nice family. Since we were dressed up to go to town, Mother felt good enough to stop in and visit with our neighbors. I liked adult conversation. You can learn a lot if you sit quietly and become invisible. My ears would perk up like an elephant's.

Canning always commenced the next day before the produce lost its freshness. Not only did we eat this food over the next few months but Mother also used the canned foods for bartering to pay our help throughout the year. She stretched a dollar like it was made of rubber.

Mother had an added hardship in that she washed our clothes outside. Next to the shop was a concrete slab where she had her wringer washing machine and two metal stands for the galvanized washing tubs. Clothes were put into the washer, where the agitator sloshed them back and forth in soapy, cold water. Then she fed them through the wringer. You had to be careful to not get your fingers caught. Mother said large-breasted women had accidentally gotten their breasts caught in the wringer, but I didn't have boobs big enough to worry about that. Flipping the lever, you'd wring the clothes through the greedy rollers to the other tub of cold rinse water and then wring the clothes dry once more. It was all right in warm, dry weather, but during cold, rainy days, it was a messy, wet, miserable job.

Mother often got way behind on her washing and ironing, so she'd go and pick up Eliza to come and help us. Eliza always made it look like fun and sometimes let me help her hang out the clothes on the clothesline. We were always on the lookout for W.A. and his tricks. He was such a bad boy, she said, and I was such a good girl.

Chapter 19

TENNESSEE, ST. SIMONS, AND THE BLUE CAR

*D*addy worked for Babcock & Wilcox in Brunswick. It was an old company that started in the mid-1800s and at first designed water-tube boilers. Their technology brought them into the nuclear age, and they helped to make the nuclear submarine USS *Nautilus*.

In 1956 Daddy was asked to work at the Oak Ridge National Laboratory in Harriman, Tennessee. The aptly nicknamed Atomic City was built in a nearby valley to house workers of the original Manhattan Project. Daddy wasn't able to find us a place to live in this futuristic city. All that he could find was an apartment attached to an old grocery store. It was awful! It sat perched on a hillside, and the back had an extremely steep slope. A busy mountain road ran past the front of the store and apartment. There was no backyard or front yard—nothing! W.A. and I did escape to the beautiful woods on the hillside to play. We'd hike up and down the hills, having great adventures, while Vera preferred to stay home and read. She was much smarter than the two of us.

We were not only packed into the apartment like workers in a sweat-shop—we also had rats. Big ones! They lived under the floor, and you could hear them scratching, running, and dancing at night with their awful squeals. Someone must have radiated them, turning them into super rats.

There was plenty of talk around the dinner table about rats, nuclear bombs, and radiation. The USSR's communist dictator, Nikita Khrushchev, was the biggest rat. He had us all afraid that Russia was going to nuke us.

Daddy called his workplace the Ridge, because the plants were located along two huge ridges, and if any one of the plants blew up, it would be like the atomic bomb that we dropped on Japan. We'd be toast.

Daddy was an expert welder and card-carrying union man. He welded tubes onto boilers, and then a team of experts x-rayed his welds to make certain there were no leaks. The materials he worked with were very expensive, and he wasn't allowed to make any mistakes. Now that's pressure!

Daddy made a lot of money that year. We paid off our debts and bought a new car. He stayed sober for the most part. He only went nuts near the end and was then let go, once again. This time we were actually happy that he got fired. I hated living there because there was nothing to do and nowhere to go. We couldn't wait to get home to our little house on Broadway at St. Simons Island.

We all calmed down, and life went back to normal. W.A. got a part-time job at Sam Cofer's gas station at The Pier. Working at the station gave him a sense of independence. Sam became a mentor to W.A. and was a good influence on him. W.A. loved Sam like a second father, and he worked hard to live up to Sam's standards. I'm sure it kept W.A. from becoming a thug, as that's where it looked like he was heading before he met Sam.

By then I had become a young lady. I now had a chauffeur, W.A., and an assistant chauffeur, John Robert. They both had turned sixteen and gotten their drivers' licenses and could drive the old blue car since we had a new one. John Robert's father was a cook at the Cloister, and his mother, Winnie, worked as a waitress at the yacht club. They worked long, hard hours.

John Robert was skinny and short with black hair and a squeaky voice. W.A. sometimes called him Weasel. He was a lonely, quiet kid and was always very kind to me. John Robert usually had lots of pocket money, and we (W.A. and I) helped him spend it since we didn't have very much. Gas was our only concern. Often I had to fork over some of my babysitting money for gas. Now that I had these fancy chauffeurs, I didn't have to walk anymore—I had service at the drop of a hat.

I would sit in the backseat rolling around as W.A. drove down the road, turning corners on two wheels. Down to The Pier and to the Casino we would fly! Now the boys were interested in girls, and W.A. had a huge crush on a girl named Jingle. Cruising Mallery Street, he'd look everywhere for just a glimpse of her. It drove John Robert and me nuts. We would try to convince him that she wouldn't give him the time of day, but he wouldn't listen. W.A. would also get on the airport strip and see how fast he could go without getting caught by the cops. If Mother and Daddy only knew how he drove that car.

One day I looked out our back door, and there was a white race car with a blue stripe sitting down at the shop. I think it was a Porsche. The owner, a very handsome young guy, was having Daddy repair his fender. All the neighborhood kids came around to get a close-up look at his car. We all knew how dangerous car racing was and remembered the day when someone came and told us the actor James Dean had been killed in a car accident. The owner of the car allowed us to sit behind the steering wheel. What a thrill!

The next day we all piled into the back of Daddy's truck to watch the sports car races being held at the airport. A racecourse had been set up on the abandoned airstrips. There were many race cars of different types, and we all rooted for the Porsche. Our driver didn't win that day, but you could tell he was having lots of fun.

It wasn't long after this race that Dr. Simmons asked W.A., along with some other young men, to be drivers for the hydroplane boat races being held at the marina. He must have witnessed how fast W.A. drove around the island. The St. Simons Boat and Fishing Club sponsored two races: one in July (a regatta) and one in August (a marathon) in the Frederica River on the intercostal waterway. We all went to see W.A. race and sat on the sandy bank under the shade of the oak trees. The river was lined with many boats, and their drivers came from different towns in the south to participate in the races. There were lots of colorful boats with engines roaring as they sped up and down the river leaving large rooster tails in their wakes. This was the early age of hydroplane racing. The boats were small but had large engines. We all could see in W.A.'s face that he got a thrill from racing. You could see the pride on Daddy's face as W.A. finished a race. Daddy was one of the first fathers to greet his son's boat as it pulled into the dock. We were all very proud of him.

I loved the thrill of racing and fast cars too.

"You taught W.A. to drive when he was only thirteen. Why won't you teach me? I'm almost thirteen now. You always tell me to act my age and grow up, but you won't let me. It's not fair!" After much nagging, Daddy gave in.

I was out of the house in an instant and seated in the car, ready to go before Daddy could even get up from his chair. He came outside, and I was so ready I had chills going up and down my spine. I was going to drive! Daddy stood there looking at me for a minute.

"Get out of the car," he said. My heart sank. Oh no, he had changed his mind. He motioned for me to come over to him.

"Come 'ere. I got to explain something to you first." He squatted down and, using his finger, drew an *H* in the sand.

"OK, this is where first is. Then across the bar and up to second. Then, down here is third. To go in reverse you go back up, across the bar, and then up to reverse."

I got that down pat. We climbed into the car, and he explained three pedals: the clutch (left foot), the brake, and the gas (right foot).

"When you press the gas pedal, pretend there is an egg underneath and push it gently. The left hand goes on the steering wheel, and the right hand goes on the gearshift."

"Easy. I got it. The letter *H*, three pedals, and a steering wheel. Nothing to it."

I turned on the ignition, put the lever in gear, and down the road that car hopped, skipped, jerked, and jumped. I didn't take a straight route but veered off the sides of the road, running over small bushes and dodging the neighborhood kids. We finally got to the end of the road, and Daddy disrupted me by yelling, "Brake!" I stomped my right foot to the floor, making Daddy's chin nearly hit the dashboard, but we had stopped.

After collecting my thoughts and recovering from him yelling at me, I tried getting the car in gear to back it up. It took me forever, and Daddy wasn't helping. He made me figure it out by myself. He giggled and giggled at me like this was the best entertainment he'd had in years until I finally worked it out. He stopped smiling when I proceeded driving again, both in and out of the road. Finally, we arrived back home. Daddy opened the car, got out, and motioned for me to go ahead and drive down the street. Mother was sitting on the porch.

"Bill," she called out, "you're not going to let her drive by herself."

"Yes, I am. I'm not going to let her kill me," he said with a chuckle.

I took off again in the car, hopping, skipping, jerking, and jumping down Broadway. At the end of the road, I was having trouble finding reverse gear. I sat there trying to get that shift in the right place for what seemed like an hour. Finally I slipped the car into the right gear and drove back to the house. Daddy came back out, got into the car, and went over his instructions with me again. By the time I walked into the house, I was totally rattled.

Mother asked, "Where is your driving instructor?"

"He's out there sitting in the car. I think he has a bottle under the car seat because I saw him take a little nip."

"What?" She went out to the car, and he was passed out. "Bill, wake up! Get in the house! All of the neighbors will see you." She just shook her head with disgust and walked back into the house.

"Carol, your instructor is apparently taking a nap!"

I grabbed my camera and said, "Mother, I want a picture of this!" I stood on the porch and took a picture of him slumped over in the passenger seat thinking *what kind of driving instructor is this?*

Daddy "napping"

Chapter 20

JEKYLL ISLAND TURTLE EGGS

One gorgeous day in early June, Daddy took the family for an outing to Jekyll Island. We launched our boat from the St. Simons Marina and made our way down the Frederica River into St. Simons Sound. As we passed The Pier and the lighthouse, we went south and landed on the beach at Jekyll Island. It was so very beautiful!

We started walking down the white sand beach and came upon some tracks. Daddy reminded us it was the season when loggerhead turtles would be laying their eggs. He said, "Why don't we follow these tracks to see if a turtle has laid her eggs?"

Could these tracks be from the turtle that my daddy saved by repairing its shell? Earlier that year Daddy arrived home with a turtle in the back of the truck. A fisherman caught it in his net, and the turtle had been injured. The neighborhood kids all came over to see the giant turtle. Each kid took a turn spraying it with water to keep it cooled off while Daddy tried to figure out a way to repair its shell. He patched it by attaching a metal clip through the shell and added bonding material. Later we all loaded into the truck and headed out to the Coast Guard station beach. We drove the truck right down close to the water and parked. Then, all hands together, we lifted the giant sea reptile out of the truck bed and released it at the edge of the water. It was very exciting to see the turtle swim away and know that we'd had a hand in its recovery. Somehow we'd established a bond with this wild creature, and when it dragged itself into the waves and swam out toward the deep, we all clapped and yelled, "Yay!" Best of all was that my daddy was the hero of the day.

Walking up to the nest, Daddy yelled, "Damn raccoons! They've dug up these turtle eggs. Let's try to cover them back up."

We scrambled around and collected all the eggs that had not been eaten. I picked one up for a quick examination. It felt like a soft Ping-Pong ball.

"Hey, these would make good falsies."

I slipped it under my swimsuit top and picked up another egg. I positioned them into place where I should have had boobs by now. I strutted around for a minute or two, delighted with my new femininity and yelled to Daddy and Mother, "Hey, look. I have breasts!"

"Carol, get those eggs out of there and into the nest," Daddy said. "Those baby turtles will hatch in a minute and nip off your little nipples." I snatched them out of my suit real quick and placed them in the nest. While packing them in tightly, I couldn't stop thinking about my nipples being bitten off. I suddenly felt quite content with my wee breasts just the way they were.

After repairing the turtle's nest, we strolled down the beach, picking up shells and enjoying the beautiful scenery. We found a large driftwood tree that had washed up on the beach. The limbs made a great place for us to sit. Daddy had packed a special picnic lunch—Vienna sausages, pork and beans, soda crackers, sardines, moon pies, and Cokes. While we ate, Daddy told us stories about our island during World War II, when planes, blimps, and even men on horseback patrolled the coastline looking for German submarines. He said the Germans sent submarines to drop off saboteurs and spies. German U-boats cruised along our coastline blowing up ships, and the spies and saboteurs were dropped off on Jekyll Island to try to blow up the shipyard and navy base. It never happened of course, but one spy was caught in 1942 on Jekyll Island. His name was Christopher Hoffman, and they put him in a POW camp in North Carolina. Daddy said that the whole time he worked at the shipyard and the navy base he worried these Nazi saboteurs might blow them up.

Next Daddy told us the legend of Blackbeard Island. Blackbeard was a pirate who conducted raids on ships a long time ago. The story goes that he buried his treasures on an island north of Sapelo, Blackbeard Island, but they'd never found any treasure there. It could be on Jekyll, St. Simons, or any one of the islands. Our eyes were popping out at that. There could be buried treasure anywhere!

Mother explained to us about the historic cottages on Jekyll that had belonged to the wealthiest people in America, like the Rockefellers and Vanderbilts. They lived in the lap of luxury there during the winter months. They called it the Jekyll Island Club, and their guests stayed at a beautiful Victorian-style hotel. Eliza once told Mother that one of her relatives used to row a boat from St. Simons to Jekyll to work at the hotel as cook.

Daddy had us riveted to that spot on the sand, listening to all of his stories. I looked at W.A.'s, Vera's, and Mother's faces, and they all looked so happy. Why couldn't it be like this all the time?

Chapter 21

VERA

*V*era and I became much closer after Betty got married and moved away to West Virginia. We shared a small bedroom that was just big enough to hold the pretty twin beds and matching dresser that

Mother purchased for us from a used-furniture store. Our room had no air-conditioning or window fan in the summer and no heat in the winter. Because the kitchen was located next to our room, when mother was cooking, it felt like it was 150 degrees in our room. I really don't know how Vera stood the hot weather, because she let me have the bed next to the window. When it was sweltering hot, she would push my bed up to the window so that I could put my pillow in the windowsill and catch what little air movement there was from outside. Then, in the winter we would shiver from the cold. Mother would pile heavy quilts on us.

As much as Vera made me feel I was special to her, it wasn't a perfect situation for either of us. She was a teenager, and I was her bratty little sister. Most of the time, we got along quite well, but her mood swings were hard for me to understand. It was hugs and kisses one minute, and the next minute she wouldn't even look at or speak to me.

Vera helped with household chores so that mother would have time to sew. Mother had a rule: no sewing unless the house was cleaned up and her nails were perfectly manicured. If you wanted new clothes, you had to work for them. She had an old treadle-style Singer sewing machine that she could just make hum. What beautiful clothes she made for us! She spent hours sewing, basting and fitting. She would rip the seams out and start all over if they didn't fit to perfection. Mother took lots of pride in her sewing. Eliza would come on occasion to wash and cook, giving Mother more time to sew. I helped too. I was the dishwasher.

Vera was also my protector. When Daddy would start drinking and become abusive, she'd slip me out of the window to safety and down to the shop. Sometimes the shop would be unlocked and we could hide inside, but if not, we'd find a place behind the shop. It's funny, isn't it, how when you're running for your life, snakes, lizards, and the darkness of night are of no concern?

Mother said Vera was most like Daddy. Both of them had trouble expressing their feelings. She always sat next to him or tried to get his attention, but most of the time, he just ignored her. Vera managed to separate Daddy in her mind into two different people—the good daddy who didn't drink and the bad daddy who did and who caused so much pain to all of us. I guess it worked for her, and maybe W.A., but it didn't work for me. He was who he was—our father.

Vera was getting more and more attention from the boys. When she took me to the pool, the boys' eyes would almost pop out at the sight of her. She had a sultry, sophisticated look and could instantly transform her sixteen years into twenty-five and look like Jane Russell. She could walk like Marilyn Monroe and had just as good a figure. Vera could have been Miss America; she was a knockout and had the brains to go with it, too. Girls used to pay her money to do their math and to write book reports for them.

Vera loved to read romance novels and go to the movies. She was in love with love. She took me to movies that I probably shouldn't have seen—movies like *Roman Holiday*, *An American in Paris*, and *East of Eden*. She was a big fan of James Dean. My favorite love story was *Lady and the Tramp*, and Mother made sure that I got to see all of the Disney movies.

Movies influenced our sense of fashion. Mother was furious when Vera bought a pair of stiletto heels. They were not at all practical, but Vera did look beautiful in them. I bought sexy flats just like Audrey Hepburn's, and they were quite stunning. When movie stars began wearing capris, we had Mother make us some.

Vera started dating at sixteen, and I became her official chaperone. The Island Drive-In Theater wasn't far from our house. The only way Vera could go there with a date was to take me. They would try to slip me in without paying for me, but Mrs. Tashati was no dummy. That large lump in the backseat covered with a blanket couldn't hold the giggles back, so it was a dead giveaway. "Is that you, Carol?" she'd say. Then when I confessed, she'd turn to my sister's date and say, "That will be an extra fifty cents." Once he handed it over, we were admitted.

We'd drive down the sandy lane to where the projection booth was located. The car would stop, and Vera's date would say to me, "OK, kid, get out and sit there on that bench until I pick you up." Then they would drive off. I'd join the other kids who had been dumped off for the same reason. Actually, it was on that bench that I had my first kiss. I will never forget it. A really cute boy named Paul was sitting on the bench one night, and three girls held him down so that I could kiss him. He was not happy at all.

Once I got upset because a kid was picking on me, and I needed to find Vera and her date. I didn't know where they had parked, so I started looking into cars, trying to find them. Some of the windows were so steamed up that I couldn't see inside the cars they belonged to. I sure did scare a lot of people that night. Suddenly the girl would scream, "Who's that staring through the window?" The next thing I knew, she'd be scrambling around and pushing the boy away, and her date would yell at me, "Get lost, kid!" I finally did find the car my sister was in, and I scared them too. Vera's date was not happy to see me, but he gave me money to buy refreshments and sent me back to the bench. I loved being Vera's chaperone.

One day Mother caught Vera smoking in the bathroom. It was a tiny room outside the kitchen, and you got to it by walking through the screened porch. On cold days nobody stayed in there any longer than they had to; we'd get back into the warm kitchen as soon as we could. Maybe that was how Mother realized what Vera was up to.

Mother didn't yell very often, but when she did, we stood at attention. This day, when Vera walked back into the kitchen with that meek look on her face, Mother was in a rage.

"You've been sneaking around smoking and stealing money out of my purse to buy cigarettes. Money has been missing from my change purse where I keep the quarters for your lunch," she yelled. "I've had it with you! I just can't take it anymore! Your brother is doing the same thing. I've had it! Smoke—go ahead. I just don't care anymore."

My brother and I were sitting at the kitchen table, happy to witness this big fight. We were shocked by our mother's performance. Smoking and stealing would have been a hanging offense in our house. We were even more shocked when she pointed her finger at both of us and said, "You two can smoke too!"

My mouth flew open as I said, "Really?"

"Yes. Really."

Wow, I could smoke if I wanted to. I couldn't wait to tell my friends. I guess Mother was trying some kind of reverse psychology on us, or she was just joking when she gave us permission to smoke. W. A. took her at her word and started smoking, but not in front of Mother and Daddy. He had a clear conscience.

Soon after Mother raged at Vera, I headed over to my friend Cree Grey's house to play. I had been venturing farther and farther from my old friends on Broadway to new friends on Demere Road. I walked down Broadway, turned left on Demere, and made my way to the curve where the Battle of Bloody Marsh Monument stood. There was a little ledge on the monument where I would often sit and gaze into the marsh, remembering the scary ghost stories that Vera would tell all of us. She told us how the Spanish soldiers were killed by Oglethorpe's men at that spot. She said that their blood oozed out of those dead soldiers and into the marsh, and at certain times the blood would come to the surface. Vera also told us a ghost story about another place on the island where slaves had once been brought onshore at Dunbar Creek and how they drowned themselves. Rather than submit to slavery, they marched chained together as their leader led them into the water. She told us that at night you could still hear their chains rattling and their moans as they walked into the water drowning themselves. Even Eliza said it was a spooky place and she would not go there. Vera could tell really scary ghost stories that seemed almost real.

I continued south to the corner of Demere and East Beach Causeway to my friend Cree's house. It was a beautiful two-story, red-framed house.

The boy who lived next door to Cree was named George Stephens. George also had a nice house, which backed up to the marsh. His family had a long boardwalk dock that led down to the little creek, where he had a clubhouse. At high tide the shack was surrounded by water. George asked Cree and me if we wanted to smoke.

"Well, yeah! My mother says I can smoke if I want to."

The three of us went into the clubhouse, and George brought out a bag he had hidden beneath one of the benches. Inside the bag were a Sears catalog, matches, and some weed-like stuff. He took one of the thinnest pages of paper from the catalog, tore it into smaller pieces, and handed each of us one. I had seen my father roll cigarettes before, and it looked easy. When Daddy had a job, he smoked Chesterfield, and when he didn't, he rolled his own cigarettes with Prince Albert tobacco, which came in a pretty red tin that we could keep marbles and trinkets in.

We struggled with rolling the tobacco evenly in the paper strips, but eventually we had things that resembled cigarettes. We all lit up and started puffing away. Camels or Lucky Strikes couldn't possibly have been any better. We puffed and puffed away, having a great time. Suddenly, a wave of nausea hit me; from head to toe, I started to feel weak and giddy.

"Am I turning green?" I asked. Then a huge wave of nausea rose up from that place God calls hell, and it nearly bowled me over. Jumping up, I ran out of the clubhouse and down the dock, looking for a good place to throw up. I leaned over the rail and puked and puked. When I stopped retching, I looked back, sorrier than a sick dog, and waved good-bye to my friends. I just wanted to get home to my mother, and I ran as hard as I could.

As soon as I reached my house, I made a beeline for the kitchen sink. I continued to puke, splashing cool water on my face between sessions that nearly turned me inside out. When my insides were scoured of everything they had held, I drank water and puked that up too. Mother came in and looked at me like she was real worried.

"What have you been doing?"

"You said that I could smoke if I wanted to. Oh, Mother, I'm sooooo sick!" Her face changed from worry to something with a lot less empathy. She laughed and got me a cold washcloth to put on my face.

"You might have smoked something poisonous. I'd better call Mrs. Grey and see if she knows what was going on."

That's how Mother found out that we'd been smoking rabbit tobacco. All I can say is that it was nasty stuff. I could tell Mother was no longer concerned because, after talking with Cree's mother, she turned her head the other way and snickered every time I threw up.

Mother made me go to bed. I was so sick; I thought I was walking to my deathbed. I assured her that she didn't ever have to worry about me spending my lunch money on cigarettes. I swore to God that if I got through this alive, I would never, ever smoke again. And I didn't.

In 1956 Vera met a very handsome sailor from Washington State. He was the best-looking guy I had ever seen, and he even took time to have conversations with me. It was only a couple of weeks after Vera met him that she and Mother were planning a wedding. Vera was crazy in love—a whirlwind romance, just like in the movies.

Vera and Ron had a lovely little wedding with a reception at our house. I even got a store-bought dress and new shoes.

For a couple of months, they rented a small apartment in Brunswick, and then later Ron was shipped out to California. They packed their bags and were on their way. I now felt like this sailor had shanghaied my sister. I thought I would never see her again. I loved her and missed her terribly. The empty space in our room was devastating, and every time I went in there, all I could think of was my sister's face blurring through my tears as they drove away. Vera couldn't come home to visit very often because it was too expensive to fly from California. It was like she had disappeared from my life. After Vera moved, I became very lonely and depressed because we had always been together. Now there was no one to talk to, no more dates, and no one to protect me. I was on my own.

Chapter 22

JAY—THIRTEEN YEARS OLD AND THE
VALENTINE'S DANCE

*I*n the fall of 1957, I was enrolled in Glynn Middle School. I now had to ride the bus to Brunswick along with all the island kids in grades seven through twelve. The bus would park at Brunswick High School to load and unload all of the students, and the middle school students had to walk across the street, through the high school campus, and across a large field to their school. I thought that I was all grownup, but a few seniors let me know real soon that I was no match for them. They bullied me often by not letting me have a seat next to them or by just teasing me, telling me that I had cooties.

I had a classmate named Jay who would save me a seat on the bus when he could. We became boyfriend and girlfriend. He was my first heartthrob. He was very smart and keenly interested in science. His father worked at Thiokol and was involved in making rockets. Jay's father used to help him make and launch water rockets in their front yard. Jay would invite all of the neighborhood kids to watch his launches. We'd be in awe of the rockets' power; the dizzying heights they reached in the sky were far beyond anything I ever thought a kid could achieve.

Also, Jay had a paper route and delivered papers in my neighborhood. Every day after school, he would come to my house on his bicycle and pick me up to help him deliver the newspapers. I would ride with him on his bike and toss the papers into the yards. Off we'd go, delivering papers down Broadway and back up First Avenue, over to Frederica Road. Then we'd stop at all of the stores and bars. We'd go into the Oasis and grab a handful of peanuts off the bar. I would always check to see if my daddy was sitting there drinking. We loved to listen to the washboard band that played there, and on occasion we'd stand outside the door to hear them play. We didn't hang around long because the bartender would shoo us away. Then we'd continue on our route delivering papers and checking the last bar, Pete's Place, to see if my daddy happened to be there.

Our last paper delivery was at the green house where a black family lived. This wasn't just any house. It was the house owned by Jasper Barnes, the great-grandson of Neptune Small. Neptune had purchased a large tract of land that is known today as Barnes Plantation. Jasper and his brother William were well known because they owned two very successful night-clubs frequented by black patrons—the Blue Inn Club and the La Quartz Club. Of all of Jay's newspaper customers, the Barnes family was the most generous. They always gave Jay a tip when they paid their bill. As kids, we thought that they were really rich.

The last delivery was at the Island Drive-in Theater, where we'd stick a newspaper inside the ticket booth. We'd quickly make that last delivery so that we could make our last and favorite stop. Now, with money and our pockets full of peanuts, we'd stop at the SOC gas station to get a Coke. Jay always had enough money to buy me a Coke. He often joked about all the money he was making delivering newspapers. Then he would take me back home. We'd say our good-byes while anticipating seeing each other the next day on the school bus. I couldn't believe it. I actually had a very cute boyfriend!

February rolled around, and Jay invited me to the Valentine's dance at school. I was so excited. Mother started making me a party dress. She spent hours and hours sewing. We went to town and bought party shoes for me too.

Only a few days before the dance, Jay informed me that he couldn't take me because his mother had arranged for him to go with the daughter of one of her friends. I was devastated! Mother insisted that I go to the dance anyway. She assured me that I wouldn't be the only one without a date.

My father dropped me off at the front door of the school, and I went inside, where I stood against the wall like all the other wallflowers. I was miserable. Then I saw Jay walking in with this redheaded girl in a green taffeta dress. She was kind of pretty. It just broke my heart. He was my first boyfriend and now he has broken my heart. I was so deeply saddened to see him with another girl.

As soon as Jay saw me, he came over and left the red-haired girl just standing at the door. He asked me to dance. We were awful dancers, but we laughed and were having fun. Both of us totally forgot about the red-haired girl that night. Soon the dance was over, and our parents picked us up to take us home.

The next day Jay told me his parents were extremely angry with him and that they'd said he couldn't see me or have anything to do with me anymore. I was shocked! I was so angry with Jay's parents. It was true that we had hurt someone, but I could sense that there was much more to it.

That evening while sitting at the dinner table, my brother explained to me, "He can't see you anymore because you are from the wrong side of the tracks."

Puzzled, I said, "W.A., that's so stupid! St. Simons doesn't have trains or railroad tracks."

As Mother got up from the table, she sadly patted me on the head and remarked, "You have a lot to learn."

And learn I did.

Jay got another paper route and no longer saved me a seat on the school bus. It wasn't long before he moved away. It broke my heart the way his parents had treated me. I felt a pain that I had never experienced before: a feeling of deep rejection. My next-door neighbor Johnny wasn't allowed to talk to me and now Jay! Maybe my grandmother was right—Daddy's sins were my sins. I felt totally worthless.

Fourteen years later, a major accident happened at Thiokol Chemical Corporation's Woodbine plant, where Jay's father used to work. It was 10:53 a.m. on Wednesday, February 3, 1971, when a devastating blast leveled a magnesium-flare assembly building. A security guard at the entrance gate, two miles from the site of the blast, said it looked like an atomic bomb had exploded. Twenty-four people lost their lives in the blast. Some of the victims were dismembered, and of these, five died in the coming days. More than fifty workers were injured, and many of them spent months in hospital.

When I heard about it on the news, I feared that Jay's father might have been killed or injured. At the same time, it brought back all of those feelings of anger toward his father. I felt ashamed for my anger, and I prayed that Jay's father was OK.

The pain I suffered from being treated like I wasn't good enough was something that I could, and eventually did, get over, but Jay will never be forgotten—he was my first love.

With my new realization that we were not all equal in other people's eyes, I was determined to show that I was as good as anyone. It didn't matter if I was born on the wrong side of the tracks. If they didn't want to be with me, it was too bad for them. It was their loss, not mine. Maybe this was the point in my life when I started growing up knowing that my parents could no longer protect me from the outside world. It was now about me and who I was going to be in life. It hurt deeply to feel inferior to certain other people because of circumstances that I had no control over. I had been put in my place. It wasn't a little tap on the head. I had been hit by a two-by-four. The playground had gotten bigger and tougher. I had to learn to protect myself and my feelings.

Chapter 23

GERALD

*I*t was late summer when my father came home with a new seine (or drag) fishing net, about twice the size of his old one. He couldn't wait to go out and test it. He wanted to catch some shrimp for dinner, or maybe a couple of fish would be nice, but the main purpose was to catch a good supply of mullet as bait for fishing for bass. Daddy called his close friend Gerald, who lived only a few doors up the street, to ask if he wanted to go seining at East Beach. Gerald was married to a really wonderful lady named Faye, and they had two children. W.A. called several boys from the neighborhood and invited them to go with him. I asked Daddy if I could go too. He looked at me for a minute and then gave me fair warning that if I went, I would have to hold up my part of the net.

"If I let you come with the boys, I don't want to hear a single complaint. You got that?" I nodded with a show of as much confidence as I had in me.

"Go hop in the truck then." As I ran out the door with a whoop, his voice followed me. "And don't make me sorry I brought you along."

Daddy and Gerald loaded the net into his old, trusty blue truck, and all the kids jumped into the back of the pickup. We drove to Gould's Inlet on East Beach; then all hands, including mine, helped to carry the heavy net down the dunes and onto the beach. Our first job was to untangle it and lay it flat on the sand. Each person was assigned a section and told to hold on to the rope at the top of the net.

"When I give the word, I want you all to hold your section up. Then we're going to walk the net, one at a time, into the water. No horsing around! Anyone who can't follow orders or doesn't think he or she can keep up with the others goes home now—got it?"

Daddy took hold of his end and led the crew, step by step, section by section, out into the ocean. Gerald and I were the last ones to enter the water, Gerald behind me, holding the end of the net as we walked farther and farther from the shore. The idea was to go out as far as we possibly could and then make a big sweep back to the beach. I held my position quite well, but whenever a wave came along, I struggled to stay above the water. Pretty soon I was in over my head, just holding on to that rope as hard as I could and swimming to maintain my position with the others.

Soon Daddy yelled, "Sweep the net back to the beach." He started to drag his end of the net back toward the shore, and as we followed his path, the net closed in on the trapped fish. I couldn't see but felt things slide across my skin, scamper around, and bump into the front of my body, some making pretty hard contact in their panic. It soon dawned on me that there could be sharks trapped in there along with the fish and shrimp that were now hitting against me with increasing frequency.

Suddenly something grabbed me from behind; it pulled me backward like it was consuming me. But this was no shark. These were the arms and hands of a man. They reached around me, grabbed my tender little breasts, and squeezed. They squeezed so hard. They slid down my belly and slipped into my shorts, while the arms held me in a crush. The body behind me was hard and purposeful—a machine with no heart—and it curled around me. A hand—a big hand—pushed between my legs and dug into me, and fingers touched me in a place and in a way no one had ever touched me before. This was so wrong, and this was Gerald! I was in shock. I tried to push away from him, but a large wave crashed over my head, and he had me trapped, just like the fish in the net.

Gerald pushed my head under the water and kept me there while he assaulted my body. I needed air, and I needed to get away from his hands and arms. I panicked. Kicking and flailing, I used every ounce of strength I had to escape his grip, but he held me under the water. I was no match for his strength. I continued my struggle, doing everything I could to escape his grip.

All of a sudden it stopped. His arms released me, and I popped to the surface. When I opened my eyes and looked around, Gerald was gone. I started swimming for shore.

"Oh my God, Daddy will kill him for sure if he finds out," I thought. "I mustn't say anything." I made it to shore, coughing and spitting up water. I walked onto the beach with my head bowed down, quiet and withdrawn. I had further humiliation to endure when the boys started taunting me. "Ha-ha! You're a sissy girl and couldn't hold up your part of the net. Na, na, na, na na..."

Daddy didn't look at me. Neither did W.A. They focused on their tasks of storing the catch and folding the netting. I turned my back on all of them, sat on the beach, and just gazed out across the ocean. I didn't cry. I took one huge breath, and I held it all in.

From that day on, if I saw Gerald anywhere near or around my house, I left. I was terrified of him. Just the sight of him made my heart pound so hard and so loud that I feared my secret would be given away. Waves of nausea would then threaten to overcome me. If it had happened to me once, it could happen again. I lost total interest in fishing for fear that Gerald might go with us, and because of this situation, I hated my father. My only concern was staying out of Gerald's grasp. It seemed I was perfect bait for this type of man.

Chapter 24

HOW MUCH?

One day I heard machinery clearing lots over on First Avenue. I walked down the street to see the destruction of the thick, spooky section that I had always hated when walking home at night. Soon construction began, and oh, how I loved seeing these new homes being built. I'd pass by them at least once a day as I went to school or on one of my adventures. Mr. Williams, the developer, was going to rent these houses out to people, and I wondered if any of the families would have kids my age.

When the houses were finished and looked about ready to rent, I went over and asked Mr. Williams if he was interested in hiring me to help him clean up the trash. He told me no, but asked if I would consider sweeping out the rooms.

I said, "Sure. That would be fine. All three?"

"Yes."

The floors were terrazzo tile, concrete mixed with colorful stone flakes that were then sanded smooth. The floors were now covered with dust. He handed me a broom, and I started sweeping.

The first house went OK. After the second house, my hands were getting a little tender. As I swept out the third house, I was beginning to think that I couldn't finish. Big blisters covered my hands, and they really hurt.

I was determined to finish the last house though, and so I did. I went over to where Mr. Williams was working and said I was finished. We walked through each room of all three houses for a final inspection.

"OK," he said. He reached into his pocket, pulled out a handful of coins, scratched through them, and then handed me a quarter. My heart sank. What? That couldn't be true. I thought I would earn enough money to buy anything I wanted at Palmer's five-and-dime store. My little blistered hand clutched the quarter, and I spun around, not saying a word. I bolted out of there as fast as I could, raced home, ran onto the porch, and threw the screen door open. As I rushed into the kitchen, tears streaming down my face, I found Mother standing at the sink.

"Carol! What is wrong? Tell me. What has happened?" I showed her my hands. "Oh," she said, "how did this happen?"

Between sobs I managed to tell her, "I swept out Mr. Williams's three houses, and this is all he gave me!" Mother wrapped her arms around me and made the comforting sounds that only mothers can make. I could feel her indignant anger rise in her shoulders as she took in what had happened.

"You wait until your father comes home! He will go and tell Mr. Williams a thing or two. Doing this to a child is unforgivable."

Mother's tone confirmed I had been taken advantage of or, as I thought, robbed. I ran into my bedroom and lay on the bed sobbing. Soon Daddy came home, and Mother told him what had happened.

"Bill, go in there and talk to Carol."

Daddy sat down next to me on the bed. "Tell me the whole story."

"OK," I sobbed. I had reserved some of my sobbing for now, when I hoped to rile my father's sense of outrage. My daddy would show *that* man a thing or two. Maybe he'd sock him in the nose, make it hurt like hell and bleed all over the place. I told Daddy the story from beginning to end.

"OK, let's go back to the beginning. What did you agree to be paid for sweeping the floors?"

I looked at Daddy. "What?"

"What did you agree to be paid for sweeping the floors?"

"Well," I said, thinking back, "we didn't talk about that."

"Carol, you always agree on a price before you do the work."

"Oh, I didn't know that."

My father stood up, patted me on the head, and said, "Don't you blame Mr. Williams. It was your mistake. You should have agreed on an amount before you started the work."

This was one of the best lessons that I ever received. After that I had no problem asking anyone, "How much?"

Chapter 25

SYLVIA AND BOMBS

*I*t was only a few days after sweeping out Mr. Williams's houses that I noticed a family was moving into one of them, and they had a blond girl about my age. I became very excited at the prospect of having another girlfriend my age since Katie, Delores, and Brenda had moved away. I walked by the house many times, trying to find an opportunity to say hello. Finally, one day she saw me and ran out of her house to introduce herself.

"Hi. I'm Sylvia."

We hit it off immediately. She invited me into her house to meet her family. Sylvia's father, Monty, was a lieutenant commander in the navy and stationed at the Glynco naval base. I thought he looked like Clark Gable with his mustache and cute smile. Mrs. Montgomery was beautiful. Her name was Nettie. She had once been a model in California. She was always very well dressed, and her long fingernails were painted bright red. I had never seen nails that long. Sylvia introduced me to her brothers, Paul and Chris.

It wasn't long before the Montgomerys found out that my father had a drinking problem. There was an incident where Daddy was shooting his gun off in the front yard and yelling obscenities at cars as they drove by the house. No longer having our sisters at home to protect us, W.A. and I were on our own. W.A. was in particular danger because Daddy was especially cruel to him during these episodes.

The Montgomerys' house became a safe haven for me. Monty sat me down and told me that I was welcome at their house anytime, day or night. He said I was a brave and wonderful little girl and that going through all that I was would make me stronger than the average girl. He said, "You can take the high road, or you can take the low road in life, but taking the high road—no matter the circumstances—is always best. I'll guarantee you that someday you are going to have a wonderful life."

He asked me to learn the twenty-third psalm, the prayer that soldiers and sailors say when they are afraid. It would give me courage, he said. Monty showed me where it was in the Bible and read it to me.

"The Lord is my shepherd; I will fear no evil" stuck in my head immediately. Over time I learned all of the verses with Mother's help. She was relieved to know that they were a good family and that I would be safe with them.

Sylvia and I became inseparable. She went to the Catholic school, Saint Francis, and I went to Glynn Middle School. I started going to church with Sylvia and her family, and since Catholic women had to cover their hair in church, Sylvia let me borrow one of her many hats. My mother was OK with me going to Catholic Church, but when the Church of God deaconess Granny Hamby found out where I was going, Daddy tried to put a stop to it. I really didn't care what Granny Hamby thought. I would sneak off and go to church with Sylvia.

The Montgomerys often asked me to eat dinner with them. They ate some pretty strange stuff. I had never been exposed to Mexican, Italian, and Japanese food. I always ate what they gave me for fear of hurting Sylvia's mother's feelings and making it so she wouldn't ask me back. I made the sign of the cross just like they did and learned to say the Catholic blessing. Our family said a blessing on occasion. We took turns saying, "God is great, God is good…" but when it came W.A.'s time to say grace, he prayed, "Bless the meat, damn the skin, throw back your ears, and cram it in." Mother would be furious, but we would all break out in laughter, including Daddy.

Sylvia and her mother introduced me to *Seventeen* magazine, which was how I first learned about fashion. I had been wearing clothes just to cover my nakedness and to keep myself warm for the most part. That all changed. Sylvia would give me her old magazines, and I'd lie on my bed looking at them, over and over. I would find something that I loved and run to Mother, begging her to please make one like it for me. Mother was an amazing seamstress, cutting her own patterns out of newspaper or brown paper bags. She would shop for fabric and copy something exactly as it was in the magazine. I think she would have done anything to keep me from wearing jeans. It didn't mean that I couldn't wear jeans at all—just not all of the time.

Now Sylvia and I were fashion divas. We wanted to become Miss America. Sylvia and her mother invited me over to watch the Miss America Pageant with them. We just loved Bert Parks; he was so funny. "Here she comes, Miss America…" Sylvia and I had a long, long way to go to become Miss America. As skinny as we were, we wouldn't win any beauty contests, but we couldn't stop dreaming.

She and I had just bought matching Jantzen swimsuits—the same brand that Miss America wore in the pageant. They were hot pink and striped. We were teased about looking like watermelons. Sylvia's mother commented that at least we didn't look like zebras, like the Miss America contestants who wore the black-and-white swimsuits several years ago. We loved our swimsuits and didn't care if we looked like watermelons. We felt glamorous.

Riding horses was Sylvia's favorite sport. She took riding lessons from Mr. Long at the Sea Island Stables. I would often go with her on Saturday mornings to watch her ride. I'd sit on the fence while she pranced around the ring, and I'd help her brush the horse afterward. It hurt that we couldn't afford for me to take lessons with her, but I was still happy that I got to go to the stables and be a part of her riding experience.

One day we were playing in the ditch at my house, and Sylvia caught a little brownish-black snake. When my brother saw it, he slapped it out of her hand and smashed it. It was a baby water moccasin! Not a harmless water snake. W.A. liked snakes and caught them all of the time, so he knew what he was talking about, but Sylvia didn't believe him, so we kept the dead snake until Daddy came home. He confirmed that it was a water moccasin. He scared Sylvia even more when he told her that the snake was not only venomous but also large enough to have killed her.

Finally my mother was happy with the changes in me—I was no longer the tomboy with rolled-up blue jeans and oxford shoes. No more coon hunting for sure. I was now blossoming into a young lady. Sylvia had made a big impression on me. I had also made an impression on her by introducing her to the outdoors—playing in the woods and catching frogs, lizards, and nonpoisonous (green) snakes.

I had never had a friend quite like her. We were now little women—a most special time in a girl's life. We shared our most intimate thoughts and talked about having a boyfriend, falling in love, getting married someday, and having babies.

Not only was I enjoying my new best friend, but things at home were getting better. Then, things changed. One afternoon, Daddy came in from work and said, "Oh my God, Grace. You won't believe what I just heard." We all sat at the kitchen table on the edge of our chairs when Daddy announced to us that previous night a B-47 bomber collided with a fighter jet near Savannah. The problem was that the pilot had to drop an atomic bomb into the ocean. At that point they hadn't recovered it. There was a loud silence in that kitchen. Mother and we kids were in total shock as we tried to swallow what Daddy had just said. Here we were at our home on St. Simons Island, thinking we were safe, and now we had an atomic bomb less than a hundred miles away. Nobody said anything for a long time. I think we were trying to decipher what the situation meant to each of us. Daddy eventually explained that all of the components weren't there and it wouldn't blow up. He assured us that they had it under control and it would be taken care of.

I wasn't so sure. I was worried that the bomb would explode and I'd be radiated like those big rats under the floor in that apartment in Tennessee. I was also scared that the radiation would make me glow in the dark. Frankly, I was very uneasy about the situation.

Then he dropped his own bomb on *us* when he announced that we were moving to Huntington, West Virginia. We were going so that Daddy could help the Lushers, my sister's in-laws, with their house moving business. I was devastated by his decision. After all, I had been there with my mother before when we visited Betty. It certainly wasn't a place like our beautiful island oasis. I thought to myself that W.A. would also hate it. He would be like a fish out of water there.

All too soon, I had to leave my wonderful, beautiful friend. I was becoming an old hand at losing the people I loved, but that didn't make it any less painful. I just learned to handle it with less drama and move on.

Chapter 26

West Virginia, 1958–1959

The family was now packed and moving to Huntington. My sister Betty was very excited over us coming there. Daddy started making the new equipment for their business.

Daddy's moving-equipment designs were some of the most unique and practical solutions anyone had ever come up with. Contractors came from near and far to see what he had built. He had a great mind for this kind of thing. Mother said that during the war he played a big part in designing and making an airtight submarine door. Even though Daddy wasn't drinking as much, he didn't make very much money during this time. Times were hard for us.

We rented a small apartment over a store on Altizer Avenue. The city buses expelled strong diesel fumes into the apartment, making it almost impossible to open the front windows. The windows looked out over the street to a huge concrete floodwall. On the other side of the wall was the Guyandotte River, a tributary of the Ohio River. In the spring, the river would sometimes flood so badly that they would have to close the gates. It felt like living in a prison.

Since the apartment had only two bedrooms, I had to sleep on a mohair sofa in the living room. It was pure hell because it itched my skin to death. Mother would try to cover it, but as I tossed and turned in the night, the three cushions popped up and down, pulling the sheets and blankets away and exposing my skin to the itchy mohair.

Betty and Kenny's house was only a couple of doors away from our apartment. I spent a lot of time playing with their two precious little girls, Grace and Paula. Betty was such a wonderful mother. I was only six years old when Betty married and moved away, so I'd hardly spent any time with her. Mother had given me to Betty when I was born because she had wanted another boy. I couldn't imagine Mother wanting another boy like W.A. He was the biggest pest and teased me unmercifully. He was such a big bully. Betty still considered me her baby, and she hugged and kissed me too much. After all, I was too old for such things now. I was a teenager.

Daddy found and rescued a baby possum under a house that he was moving. Its mother was nowhere to be found. Knowing I was very upset about where we were living and that I didn't have anything to do, he brought the possum home to me. I missed the island and my friends dreadfully, but this little fellow made up for my loss.

I named him Pogo. He was so tiny he could fit into a tea cup. I put an old yellow angora sweater in a box and made it Pogo's home. I wanted it to be as soft and cozy as if it was his mother's pouch. He had the cutest little face with a very pointy nose and tiny, black, beady eyes. I fed him milk through an eyedropper, but his favorite food of all was grapes. He started growing and soon got big enough to escape from the box. Being a nocturnal creature, he'd prowl at night. I'd hear him crawling up and down the drapes and the tape on the window blinds. In the mornings, a trail of footprints was visible in the dust on the tables and floor. He'd scout the kitchen sink for anything he could find to eat and drink. Several weeks went by, and his nighttime activities began to wake up all of us. Being much bigger and a lot stronger, he trashed everything as he rambled through the apartment. Daddy put the law down and said he had to go. I had to agree. He was getting the call of the wild. We took him to a nice spot near the river and let him go. As he wandered into the underbrush, sniffing and exploring everything around him, I realized that little possum had filled a void in my life. Caring for him made me feel much better, even if only for a few weeks.

One night Mother received a phone call from a friend in St. Simons. The horrified expression on her face made it clear: this was bad news. A neighborhood child had drowned off the beach near the Coast Guard station. Apparently a group of children had walked out onto a sandbar during low tide, and when the tide came in, the current was too strong for them to get back to the beach. One of the children drowned.

At first my heart sank in sadness. Then a lightning strike of fear hit me. "Oh no. Oh God! Was it Sylvia?"

"No, it was your little friend Penny who lived on First Avenue."

I was overcome with emotions. Tears ran down my face. Mother put her arms around me and held me tight. What a horrible shock. How could such a thing happen? We knew the beach could be a very dangerous place, with the undertow and six-foot tides. Even an adult can be powerless to swim against strong riptides. But there was a devastating difference between knowing about the risk of death and experiencing the reality, the finality, of death, especially when it was someone so young who had died. It was also the first time I had experienced the death of a playmate. I was distraught for days. I shuddered at the thought of how many times I had gone out on the sandbar by myself. I could have been washed out to sea and never seen again. How foolish I had been.

I knew that I had to find something to take my mind off all the things weighing me down. I found a job cleaning houses and babysitting for a family called the Spurlocks. They had a very nice house on Altizer Avenue. Marilla's husband worked on a river barge on the Ohio River, and he would be gone for weeks. She'd often ask me to stay overnight, and I didn't mind a bit. I loved the little boy and girl; they were sweet kids. And I loved making my own money. Little did I know that Marilla was out fooling around while I was there babysitting. Her husband caught her with another man. I felt so bad about it. I really hated seeing this family break up.

We almost had our own family break up too. Mother caught Daddy seeing Venus, Kenny's cousin. She was beautiful, just like her name. Kenny's family made us leave when they found out. Mother was very upset to say the least. She did love my father and didn't condone what he had done. Why didn't she yell, beat him up, or leave him? Why was it that she never talked to us about what was going on, leaving us with no clue as to what she was thinking? Perhaps Mother thought she was sparing us the pain and humiliation, but she wasn't.

W.A. became so unhappy living there that I think he went into some kind of depression. He slept all of the time and gained lots of weight. He started hanging around with a bunch of bums who gathered at a corner store. I saw W.A. get into an awful fight there one day. This wasn't merely a high school fight. It was a full blown bloody battle. It scared me to death. W.A. soon quit school and became a thug.

W.A. and I were happy to leave West Virginia, and so was Mother. It was a very depressing place. We missed our home at St. Simons and desperately wanted to go back. Why couldn't Daddy find work there? We hoped he would when Kenny's family said we had to leave, but we were soon disappointed. Daddy announced we were moving to Smyrna, Georgia.

Chapter 27

SENIOR YEAR AND RAYMOND, 1961–1967

From Huntington, West Virginia, we moved to Smyrna, Georgia, into one of the houses at Lake Laurel that my uncle Lee had built and couldn't sell. It was a very beautiful house with a view of the lake. Mother purchased a few essential pieces of new and used furniture for the house. Although it was scantily furnished, Mother set large bouquets of wildflowers all around the house, and it looked so homey. A few months later, my uncle sold the house, so he moved us to another one in a subdivision he was developing in nearby Powder Springs.

I had been attending Campbell of Smyrna High School, where I almost completed my junior year except that I failed biology. So, it was summer school for me with six weeks of study at South Cobb High School in Austell. I just loved summer school. It was so much better than staying at home with nothing to do but go to the swimming pool in Powder Springs.

At school, I met a girl named Patsy Stedham who had been in a terrible car accident a couple of years earlier. She had hurt her leg severely which caused her to miss weeks of school. In order to be able to graduate, she had to attend summer school.

Patsy's father was a butcher who owned a grocery store a few miles up the road from our house. Her father had bought Patsy a new car and she offered to give me a ride to summer school every day. One day when she dropped me off at home, she met my brother W.A. It was love at first sight. They started dating, and again I was an official chaperone. This time the role was for real. They took me everywhere with them. They weren't very lovey-dovey, and I never saw them kiss or hug, but they did hold hands. Was this the Victorian era? Was this what dating was all about?

Summer passed by quickly, and I started my senior year at South Cobb High School. Considering the precedent my older sisters had set, it was no wonder I was surprised when I realized I could actually graduate. I hadn't met a boyfriend to run off with like Betty and Vera had.

The elementary school principal's son, Johnny Turner, rode the same school bus as me. He was a doll! He asked me out, and we went on several dates, but I didn't like kissing, and he soon dumped me. Poor me! Oh well, I could still go on dates with W.A. and Patsy, and that was exactly what I did. I was never left at home by myself on Saturday nights, and on Sundays, W.A. would take me to watch him race his 1942 Ford hot rod on the drag strip in Dallas.

Daddy had a falling-out with his brother Lee, and he started looking for work elsewhere. He soon found a job working on heavy equipment at Yancey Brothers Caterpillar Tractors in Atlanta. While there he met a young mechanic named Tebeau, and Daddy thought he might be perfect for me. Tebeau had a job as a grease monkey, a new car (with car payments), and a drinking problem! Perfect. Daddy encouraged the relationship, and Tebeau was looking for a young, innocent, stupid girl to become his wife. We were made for each other.

As soon as Daddy introduced us, we started dating on a regular basis. I had no physical attraction to this young man. I was seventeen, and he was twenty-three. He wouldn't give up with all of his carnal knowledge, and he tried everything to get in my pants. Ice-cold. The fires of hell weren't going to heat me up.

One Saturday night he asked Daddy if he could take me to Moultrie to meet his family. I didn't want to go, but Daddy insisted, and his eyes lit up with joy when I agreed to go. I had an idea of what he was thinking—marriage! The next Saturday we left early in the morning and arrived at their house in the late afternoon. Tebeau's family was very much like my own—hardworking country people. His mother made sure there was no hanky-panky that night by putting us in separate bedrooms. The next morning we had breakfast and headed home.

We drove several hours, and then Tebeau pulled off the road to relieve himself. Then he walked over to my side of the car and opened the door. I looked at him and told him that I didn't want to go to the bathroom there and that he'd have to stop somewhere else for me. He quickly shoved me over and started assaulting me. Kicking and screaming I yelled, "Get your hands off of me! My daddy will kill you! My daddy will kill you if you touch me! Tebeau! Stop it!" Over my crying and protests, he finally gave up. I didn't say another word to him the rest of the way home. I just kept thinking, "You are as evil as Gerald."

When we arrived home, Daddy was sitting in a chair watching TV. As I rushed past, I gave him a dirty look and went to my room. Mother came into my room, where I lay on the bed crying, and asked me what was wrong. I told her. Daddy also wanted to know what was wrong, but Mother didn't tell him the whole truth. She was afraid of what he might do. He and Tebeau worked together, and she didn't want there to be a conflict that might cause Daddy to lose his job.

Daddy was hopping mad with me because he had chosen Tebeau, and what could be wrong with him? He was perfect for me. But hell no, I wasn't going to let my daddy choose a man for me who was just like him! That was the end of Tebeau. Thank God! This was about the time the Russians started building the Berlin Wall in Germany, and I started building a wall between my father and me.

I was back to dating with Patsy and W.A. Things were getting more serious with them because now they had been dating for a long time. Patsy clung to me like I was a life preserver. She was scared to death that something naughty might happen between the two of them because my brother was pressuring her to get more serious. She was a very religious person and didn't believe in sex before marriage.

Christmas passed, and still I had no boyfriend. My reputation of being a cold fish must have spread around the school. If I spread my legs, I was sure to be popular, but that wasn't going to happen for fear of my daddy. He had the southern values that held women to the highest standard: rigid chastity for daughters and wives and a totally different set of rules for the men.

I was enjoying school and had made friends with some really nice girls. Several of us decided to go to the drugstore in Powder Springs to buy some valentines for school the next day. Across the street downtown was a garage where a group of guys worked on cars. They had a car club called the "Push Rods." Cute, right? One of the guys standing out front checking out the girls was Johnny Turner, my old boyfriend. He yelled and waved at me, and I responded. Raymond Gunnell, one of the older members, asked Johnny who I was.

"You won't like her. She's a cold fish."

Raymond laughed. "Yeah? I bet I could warm her up and have her for supper." Well, the bet was on.

Raymond walked across the street and asked me out. I had no idea about the bet, and all I could think was "Who is this guy?" Johnny ran across to confirm he was a nice guy and I should go out with him. "No, thanks." I went inside and shopped around for my valentines, and when I left the drug store, there was Raymond standing outside the door. What could I have said but yes?

That Saturday Raymond knocked on my front door with a huge box of candy. His shiny, black Corvette was sitting in the driveway. W.A. rushed over to the window to check out my date. He just shook his head and told Mother, "I know this guy. He's a member of the Push Rod hotrod club, and he's probably twenty-five years old!" That was a surprise to me. Raymond had such a baby face that he looked like a teenager. At the same time, no boy I knew in high school could afford a Corvette! What a big surprise to me. My father was still upset that I had broken up with Tebeau, whom my father thought was perfect. And, now, I was going on a date with an older, more mature man who he thought was slick as a whistle. He was afraid that Raymond would rob me of my virginity and then dump me.

I kept up the Victorian values for weeks and only started feeling a little spark or two with a kiss. He certainly proved to be patient. No dating was allowed except on Saturday nights. We talked a lot and were getting to know each other. I could tell that he liked me very much.

One Saturday night after our date, we stood outside the door and kissed several times. Well, that proved to be a big mistake. Daddy had been drinking heavily for several days and was in a complete stupor. When I came inside, he made some harsh remarks to me, but I ignored him and went to bed. In the middle of the night, suddenly I was on the floor with my bed flipped over on top of me. My daddy was yelling, "Whore!" and my mother was yelling, "Bill, stop!" as I scrambled to my feet.

He kept yelling, "You little whore! I'll kill you, you little whore!" and I was pleading with him to stop. He continued, "I'd rather see you dead than you being a whore!"

My mother screamed, "Run! He's got his knife! Carol, run! He's drunk!"

"I'm no whore. I'm a virgin, Daddy. I'm a virgin. Please don't call me a whore!"

Mother yelled again, "Run! Run—get out of the house!"

I dodged his intoxicated, stinking body and ran down the hall into the kitchen. There was a scuffle in the bedroom, and my mother was yelling. Then I could hear Daddy coming up the hall with my mother behind him. He confronted me again in the kitchen, flashing his knife. Mother grabbed his arm. In a flash, he plunged his huge pocketknife deep into her stomach.

"God, Bill, look what you have done!" Mother grabbed her belly and screamed, "Carol, run! He's going to kill us!"

Mother pushed him hard into the cabinet, and then she ran outside to the driveway, where I was now standing. She clutched her stomach, moaning, and blood poured through her nightgown. Suddenly a shadow appeared at the front door. Mother grabbed my hand, and we started running down the driveway and onto the road. It was pitch-black. All we could feel was the gravel under our feet to guide the way. We ran what we thought was a safe distance and stopped. Mother was clutching her stomach as the blood ran through her fingers. I reached over to touch her, and a fear came over me that was greater than the fear of my daddy. She could die out here on this road.

This was the first time one kind of fear left me only for another to consume me. We started crying in each other's arms. We looked back toward the house, and to our surprise, we saw Daddy walk out of the house and get into the car. He started backing down the driveway.

"Hurry! Let's lie down in the ditch! Maybe he won't see us."

It was so cold outside that I started shivering. We jumped into the ditch, clutching each other gently because the blood was still streaming from her body. Daddy drove the car past us, went down the road, and turned onto the highway.

"Carol, we have to get to Aunt Bonnell's or I will bleed to death."
Again, we started walking down the road with a quick pace. We got almost
to the highway when we saw Daddy coming back the other way, his bright
headlights flashing in the distance. We jumped into the ditch again and let
him pass. I didn't think our hearts could stand the pounding in our chests.
Then we turned right onto the highway and walked for more than a mile.
Mother was getting weaker and weaker, but finally we made it to my uncle
Sonny and aunt Bonnell's house.

I pounded on the door. "Help—help! Please help us!"

The door flew open, and my uncle grabbed Mother as she collapsed
onto the floor. We were both covered with blood. "Oh my God, what has
happened to you two?"

"Daddy stabbed Mother!"

My aunt quickly called an ambulance. As my mother's body lay there
on the floor, my aunt rushed into the bathroom to get towels to soak up
the blood pumping from her stomach. We all huddled over her, praying
she wouldn't die. Finally, after what seemed like an hour, the ambulance
arrived. The EMTs placed her in the back of the ambulance. They asked
if I'd like to ride with her so I climbed in and sat next to her. I held her
hand and stroked her brow. Her pale face and sad eyes just broke my heart.
During that ten-mile ride to Marietta's hospital, I feared that my mother
would die. They rushed her into surgery while I sat outside in the waiting
room. Why would my daddy have done such a thing? Mother saved my
life, and now she was fighting for her own.

Soon the police came and talked to me and made out their report.
Their questions made me relive the horror of what had just happened. My
aunt and uncle took me to their house to stay for a few days until Mother
came home from the hospital. Of course, Mother forgave Daddy again. Of
course, he never said one word to me.

The next week when I returned to school after the scandal of the at-
tempted murder, everyone at school was whispering and turning a cold
shoulder to me like I was white trash. I was so ashamed of the incident. I
cried a lot.

Mrs. Grey, my English teacher, asked me to go to the office to see the
nurse, and when I came back after class, she was very loving and held my
hand gently and caressed me. I felt like she understood a little about what

I was going through. Once, Mrs. Grey came to class with a black eye. She tried to cover it up, but I knew what it was. I could see the sadness in her eyes; it was very much like my mother's. She knew what I was going through at home. She now understood why I was often shy and withdrawn.

As a result of this incident, I was terribly depressed, and my graduation from high school was in jeopardy. I had totally lost interest in my studies. Out of concern for me, Mrs. Grey took me to see the school counselor in an attempt to put together enough credits for me to graduate. I think they must have fudged the number of credits I had a little bit. I probably wouldn't have graduated without their help and compassion.

There was extreme sadness in our house. I do think Daddy was ashamed of what he had done. He never said one word to me, and we never looked each other in the eye. I remember the nights when he would get up and I could hear his footsteps coming down the hall, his shadow passing under my door. A feeling of anxiety would come over me.

Things eventually started to settle down; Mother's wound was healing, and she began to feel a little better. I did all the housework, and I pampered her in every way that I could. After all, she had just saved my life.

Raymond soon called, and we went out on a date. It was a very emotional time for me, and I wouldn't discuss all of the details. I did not admit that my daddy had been trying to kill me. The next Saturday night, we had our date, and much to my surprise, Raymond gave me a beautiful engagement ring. I was so shocked. It was totally unexpected; after all, we had known each other for less than three months. You'd better believe that I was going to marry him.

Mother was happy for me, but I'm not sure what Daddy thought. I really didn't care. On May 25, 1962, I graduated from South Cobb High School, and on the second of June, I married Raymond at my home. The ceremony was followed by a small reception with family and friends present. Thank God and halleluiah! I was out of there.

I had no idea what I had just done.

Raymond and I went on a little overnight honeymoon just north of Marietta. We stayed at a small cabin in the mountains near Ellijay. I do think that Raymond was in love with me, but I really didn't know what love was at the time. I certainly found myself unprepared for sex. It was awful for me! I was so immature.

When we returned the next day, I felt like an injured, frightened child; I just wanted to go home to my mother. I knew this had been a terrible mistake. I had married Raymond out of desperation.

We stayed with Raymond's parents for about a month until the little ranch-style house he had purchased was ready. We settled in, and I found a job working in Austell at a men's clothing store called Lamar's Men's Store. I was soon promoted to work in the office, where I did International Shoe Company books with Mr. Lamar's accountant, Charlie Gunkel. Charlie was great to work with. We had adjoining offices with an open doorway between us so that we could communicate back and forth. He was so funny, but the smell that came from his office was unbearable. He had gas—the worst of any man I have ever known—and on top of that, he smoked cigars, thinking he was covering up the odor. I'd open the outside door of our offices to let fresh air in, and I'd ask, "What did you have for dinner last night, Charlie?" He'd laugh.

I think that Charlie's condition worsened when the Russians installed missile bases in Cuba. We were horrified at the thought of the Russians launching nuclear bombs from Cuba to the United States. Charlie was so stressed that he stayed home for almost two weeks. Thank God the situation was handled peacefully by President Kennedy and Russian Premier Khrushchev.

I started growing up and becoming a housewife, but far too soon I became pregnant. It was a total shock to me; fertility had been a serious problem for all of the women in our family. Raymond was excited because he wanted to start a family. I felt totally overwhelmed. I wasn't even sure that I wanted to be married, much less have a child.

Life moved on, and I worked up until two weeks before the baby was born. On the twenty-eighth of April, 1963, I had Todd. He was a little one: five pounds and fifteen ounces. Mother came and stayed with us to help me with the baby. She actually had two babies to take care of now—a newborn and an eighteen-year-old child, me. I was scared to death about everything having to do with taking care of this baby. How did you know when to feed him? How did you change a diaper? I cried a lot. But with Mother's help I was soon able to take care of myself and the baby.

I was shocked when Raymond told me that I had to go back to work. It had been only four weeks since I had given birth to Todd, but Raymond found that our finances demanded it. I did exactly as he told, but I hated the idea of leaving my little baby. Fortunately, I did find a wonderful single lady to keep Todd. Rachel loved taking care of children. Todd quickly became attached to her, so I felt better about leaving him.

I found a job in Atlanta in the coding department at Kemper Insurance. It was the lowest-paying job in the entire company, but it would have to do for the time being. I had a one-hour commute—which meant two hours of traveling every day—so I had little time to spend with my new baby. Raymond demanded that I keep the house clean and the meals on time. He was little help to me and refused to change diapers. I could hardly hold up under the pressure.

It was Friday, November 22, 1963, when I was returning from lunch, that our office received news that President John F. Kennedy, along with Governor John Connally, had been shot while riding in a motorcade in Dallas, Texas. A short time later, we heard the announcement: President Kennedy was dead. The whole office was in shock, and people were overwhelmed with emotions. Many people sat sobbing at their desks. We were told to go home. For several days I was glued to the television coverage of all the events that led up to the funeral of the president. It was a tragic loss.

That year, Raymond and I built a new house. He worked at the cabinet division of Pioneer Plastics, where he designed and sold kitchen cabinets. It was very profitable for him. I continued working for about two years until I had my daughter, Gayle. She was a delight to all of us. Todd loved her from the very start. He couldn't stop kissing her. I was now able to stay at home with my two children in our lovely new home. I found solace in sewing and gardening just like my mother had.

Raymond became overly possessive of me and the children. He no longer welcomed my family to our house. He was rude to them and made them so miserable that they didn't want to come back. He totally dominated me in every aspect of my life— what I wore, the friends that I chose, what I purchased at the store, and every detail of the household duties. I could do nothing without his permission. Time away from him was strictly controlled. I also was obedient to his sexual needs. He wouldn't let me use my own mind. Everything had to be his idea. In the past two years, I had enjoyed working because it gave me my own space to have freedom and self-expression. But now I was at home full-time, and he planned every detail of every day. If I strayed, there were consequences—fits of anger.

The rules were different for his family. We had frequent visits from his parents, who lived in the next town only a few miles away. We had dinner every Sunday after church with them. His mother gave me constant advice on how to care for Todd and Gayle in my home. I accepted it freely, but I missed my mother and would have enjoyed her input as well.

I was thankful for the things that Raymond provided, and yet I felt guilty that I was so unhappy. If I didn't obey, I felt like I was being a bad wife. The situation made me so miserable I didn't know which way to turn.

We soon found out that Todd was developmentally slow. Raymond had an extremely hot temper, and when he got impatient or annoyed, he was abusive. He had no patience with Todd whatsoever. He often jerked him and pushed him, and he used strong language. I had to keep Todd and Gayle close to me in order to ensure things ran smoothly. I could never relax, as I was always trying to stay ahead and on top of every situation.

Raymond and I had been married about five years when my cousin Gail called me and asked if I would help her find a job with Kemper Insurance. I made arrangements with all concerned, and then Gail and I headed to Atlanta for an appointment with my old boss. We were gone all day and got snarled up in traffic, so I was late coming home. I knew when I walked into the house and saw Raymond's blood-red face that I was in big trouble. Gail sensed it too, so she left quickly to go home. As I walked past Raymond, he grabbed me and threw me against the French doors. He took me by the shoulders and repeatedly shoved me against the panes and trim in the doors. He wouldn't stop. I finally managed to get away and run into the bedroom, but he followed me, grabbed me, and struck me several times.

The next morning I had to go see the doctor for my injuries. I had to have an X-ray for my back because he feared that some vertebrae might be damaged. My doctor was adamant that I leave Raymond immediately. "With your husband's hot temper and jealousy, I'm afraid you'll be found dead one day. I'll even give you the money to leave him." I thanked the doctor but refused his offer because I had enough money to leave. Getting permission from someone I respected was all it took. I did not want to end up in an abusive marriage like my mother. I also didn't want my children living in turmoil.

I called my cousin Gail and told her that I was leaving Raymond and what had happened after she left. I explained that I needed her help; I wanted to go home to St. Simons, but my injuries were severe enough that I couldn't drive myself. I quickly packed a few pieces of clothing for each of us, and as soon as Gail arrived, we headed south.

I telephoned Mother and told her what had happened and that I needed to get away. She explained that she and Daddy were temporarily living in Milledgeville, where Daddy was helping to build an electrical plant, and that I could stay at the house as long as I wanted. I had little money and no car, but the 1948 blue Plymouth with rusted-out floorboards was still at their house, so that's what I drove. I didn't care if I only had a horse and wagon to drive. My sister Betty, her husband Kenny, and their three children had moved to St. Simons from West Virginia. Kenny had been running his family's business, but because of a heart condition he'd had to find less stressful work. So Betty was there for me during this most trying time.

After being at St. Simons for about a week, I received a very moving letter from my pastor at the Methodist church in Austell.

```
First Methodist Church
John D. Maxwell, Minister
Austell, Georgia

June 21, 1967

Mrs. Raymond Gunnell
Broadway
St. Simons Island, Georgia

Dear Carol:
        It was after 10:00 o'clock last night that I
heard of your troubles. I am sorry and I would like
to do everything that I can to be of help, both to
you, the children and Raymond. From what I know of
the situation it is more of a one-sided issue and
that you have taken far more than the average person
would have.
```

```
     I hope you will understand that I am not tak-
ing sides with Raymond or with you, but after talking
with him last night he assumes all of the blame and
has come to realize what a heel he has been all of
your married life. He has told me in part of the rough
life he has lived from the age of eighteen years on.
     I am writing this, as I said, in the interest
of all of you and would like to talk with you when
you return to Austell, not that I want to try to per-
suade you in any way, but would like to be of help if
possible. I assure you that I am not partial in this
matter at all.
     My prayers are with you and the children and
Raymond.

Sincerely,
John D. Maxwell
```

Rather than tempt me to return, the letter only confirmed that I no longer wanted a life with Raymond. I'd had enough. "Let God or the devil deal with you, Raymond, for you have worn me out!" I thought. "God have mercy on your soul!"

A few weeks later, I went to SeaPak and got a job in cost inventory. I had my children, safe and sound, and by God Almighty, I swore that I would never go back to that man. I'd go and beg on the streets first.

In a three-and-a-half-month period, Raymond came down to St. Simons only one time to see the children and me, and he had never sent a dime for the children. His temper when he visited scared me even more. He told me that I would never make it without him and that I'd be starving and crawling back to him on my hands and knees.

A few months later, Raymond's cousin Lamar, who was an attorney in Marietta, called and asked me what my plans were. He told me that Raymond was selling our house and that he had already sold my car. I told Lamar that I was divorcing Raymond as soon as I could and that I'd sign over the house to him and give him everything. I was afraid of him. I just wanted out.

"I've been poor before, and it ain't all that bad," I said. Lamar refused to let me walk away with nothing. Thanks to him, we worked it all out, and I had my freedom.

Soon I moved back to Smyrna, rented an apartment, and got my old job at Kemper back. I sold my wedding rings to my aunt Gladys, and she signed a note for me to buy a car. Raymond was given rights to see the children on weekends, but I hated it. I feared for them every minute that they were with him, but he was their father, and I knew that in his own way he loved them.

I was now divorced with two children and a high school education. I was the first of my fifty-two cousins to get a divorce, and this was an embarrassment and humiliation to Daddy. He made only one comment to me during my separation: "Don't you ask me for anything! You made your bed; now you can lie in it."

Chapter 28

ROGER

*M*anaging a household all by myself and working full-time was hard for me. I began to get depressed on the weekends when I was alone without the children. I went to see my doctor, and he assured me that, with time and faith, I would have a better life. The talk really helped me. He asked if I had any hobbies, and I told him that I loved to paint but couldn't afford the supplies. About a week later, I found a package had been delivered to the front door of my apartment. There was a tiny note sticking out of the lid: *I expect a painting for my office someday. Hope this helps.*

I took the box inside and opened it to find a pallet box with brushes and oils. What a shock! It was from the same doctor who had given me the advice that I should leave Raymond. Some might think he had gone over the line by giving his advice. I just knew that it was ultimately my decision to start a new life, and his words and actions were a great support to me.

The children would come home on Sunday nights after visiting their father and find their mother covered with paint. They were my best critics. They loved everything that I did. Exhausted from painting all weekend, on Monday mornings, I'd quickly dress the children and rush out to drop them off at day care. Sitting in traffic during my two-hour commute, I would reflect on what I had accomplished with my painting so far and what my next self-taught lesson was going to be. This was better than a date with a handsome man! I was happy as a clam.

Kemper Insurance Company was located at 1401 Peachtree Street, Atlanta, the site of Margaret Mitchell's childhood home. The gray office building was about four or five stories high with a black marble facade. It had a black-and-white awning out front that extended out to the street and covered a wide sidewalk. Tourists could often be seen wandering around or parked out front, reading the historical marker about Margaret Mitchell.

I had now earned a promotion to the audit department, where I reviewed insurance field audits and clerked for the Kemper Insurance Plan. Customers would send in their monthly insurance payments to our office. I would post these payments to their accounts every day and then walk to the bank with the receipts in a little plastic purse. I'd cross Peachtree and go up toward Five Points and then over to West Peachtree to the National Bank of Georgia. The bank had designated an area as a small art gallery for local artists, and I would always take a minute or two to observe what was currently on display. Then I'd quickly rush up to make my deposit, and the teller would comment that I had paint on my cheek, my nose, or my ear.

"Oh gosh. I was painting all weekend." This routine was repeated over and over each week.

One Monday morning I looked more disheveled than usual, and the teller asked me to bring in a piece of my artwork because all the tellers wanted to see what I'd been painting. Great! Other than my children, no one had ever seen my work. I was scared to death to show them for fear of rejection. To my shock, they loved them. Then, to my dismay, the head teller said, "You are going to exhibit them in our gallery. We will ask the president what he thinks." Now I was more than scared to death. I was terrified. But the unsolicited opportunity to gain the slightest approval for all my hard work outweighed my fear of being told I wasn't good enough. That week I brought in a number of paintings for approval. The president loved them, and the bank signed me up for a December one-woman show. I was no longer terrified. I was thrilled.

In December I sold every painting on display. With the money from the paintings, I had enough to provide the children Christmas gifts. What a blessing. God does give you all the tools that you need. I couldn't believe it. The bank signed me up for another show in the next year. I could now call myself an artist. Since I was earning money for paintings, I was a professional artist. Wouldn't Bill Hendrix, my old mentor and artist friend, be proud of me?

I really didn't fit in with the younger women at work. We were miles apart in where we were in life. Many of them had just finished college or business school and spent every dime that they made on clothes and shoes.

Every day we all streamed out of the office and stampeded, like a herd of hungry animals, to Polly Davis Cafeteria. After lunch we'd have to run a gauntlet of good-looking young men who had outlined the sidewalk under the awning of our building and who would stare rudely and make comments about us as we walked through. Many of them were young law students who were working as claims adjusters until they passed their bar exams. The girls paraded their new clothes and pretended not to hear the whispers as they passed through. The phrases that hit my ears mostly consisted of speculation on whether I'd have sex with them. "She's divorced; she'll be hungry for it by now. She's got two kids—if you want her, you'll have to put up with them. She's been married; she'll be easy." I never let any of this bother me. I had been through a lot, and I knew I could survive most anything. I just ignored those young men, held on to my pride, and sashayed up and down the sidewalk with as much panache as my heroine, Scarlett O'Hara in *Gone with the Wind*.

I did notice one guy who was especially handsome, and he made real cute, respectfully flirtatious comments as the girls passed by. He stood six foot two inches, had dark hair, and wore braces on his teeth. How cute is that? I got butterflies in my tummy and my heart skipped a beat whenever I saw him. Whoo! What was this feeling? I had never felt it before.

I had made friends with a woman, Barbara, who was close to my age. She got married at nineteen but didn't have any children. We became very close. One Saturday she arranged for us to meet and see the movie *The Graduate*. While sitting in the theater, this six-foot-two guy with the braces came in, stopped at our row, and joined us as if he'd been invited. I just about flipped out! "What's he doing here?" I whispered to Barbara.

"He wants to see you. His name is Roger."

"What?"

"Roger Douglas."

Carol Hamby

After the movie we all had dinner together. I found him to be extremely intelligent and funny. I was totally captivated by him. We had such a good time, and I felt so comfortable with him. Roger said he would call me but we would have to keep it hush-hush at work because of the office rules. Roger had been respectful—not at all pushy—and he seemed almost shy, so I decided to take a chance with this guy. I thought, "Let's just see what happens," and then wrote my number on a napkin and gave it to him.

One Saturday morning my ex-husband Raymond came to pick up the children, and we had a huge confrontation. I was totally shaken up.

I called Roger and asked if he was doing anything. He said no and invited me to come over. He lived on the other side of Atlanta in Jonesboro. I arrived at his apartment in tears. He welcomed me inside, and we sat on the sofa, where he consoled me as I explained my situation to him. He couldn't have been nicer. It was just the reaction I needed at that moment, and pretty soon he had me laughing and forgetting all of my troubles.

Roger and his roommate had the dirtiest apartment I had ever seen. When I took off my shoes, he provided me with flip-flops, saying he was afraid I would get some dreadful foot disease. It looked like these two guys were rebelling against their mothers. Needless to say, I stayed over that night. I had fallen head over heels in love. I couldn't have been happier.

In December 1967, we started seeing each other on the weekends. We couldn't meet on weekday evenings because Roger was studying for the bar exams and we lived so far apart, and it made sense to spend two days together on one commute. I still ran the gauntlet at work with the other girls, never telling anyone about seeing Roger. It was always so funny watching him trying to keep a straight face as the guys talked about the ice princess with two children.

Late that February Kemper Insurance hired its first black clerk, Anna. She was about twenty-one years old, tall, very attractive, and a college graduate. She worked in underwriting with a sea of white workers, who sat at their desks in row after row in this huge office space. Anna certainly stood out. I soon noticed she didn't have anyone to go to lunch with, so Barbara and I asked her to go with us. After seeing that I didn't have a problem with her being black, someone in the company mysteriously moved my desk next to hers. We soon became good friends. She was delightful and a real joy to be with.

146

It was Friday, April 5. My workday routine was to get up at 6:45 a.m., dress, feed the children breakfast, and drive the one-hour commute to Atlanta. I was in love, and the children were happy. Turning on the car radio, I was shocked to hear that Martin Luther King Jr. had been assassinated. He had been shot at the Lorraine Motel in Memphis, Tennessee, the previous evening while standing on a balcony. There was a manhunt for the sniper who had assassinated him. "Oh my God," I thought, "how could someone do such a thing?" Such a leader for nonviolence, he had even won the Nobel Peace Prize just a few years earlier.

The office workers were all abuzz with conversation about what had happened. Clearly everyone was upset and didn't know exactly what to do or say. People didn't want to share certain political or racial views with others because they didn't know others' views. At the same time, a great leader had been murdered. It challenged everyone in a way he or she had never been before. Suddenly, we had a message come over the loudspeaker from the branch president of our company. He gave a moving speech expressing sympathy to the black community and to us as a whole. He then instructed us to go home until further notice. My emotions, like the others', were all over the map, from tears to fears.

I drove back to Smyrna and picked up the children at day care. I sat in front of the television watching for hours and then days as the events unfolded. Soon riots broke out in all of the major cities. Thousands were arrested. Cars, houses, and buildings were set on fire. People were racing around trying to get to their homes for safety. President Lyndon B. Johnson and others from both white and black communities called for calm. It was a most scary time.

I called my friends Barbara and Anna to see if they were OK. I asked Anna how her family and the black community were handling the death of their most prominent leader. She said everyone was devastated by the news and that they were praying for peace and calm.

The old feelings and emotions from when President John F. Kennedy was assassinated came flooding back. I just prayed that it would not be a white person who assassinated Martin Luther King Jr. Roger and I agreed to stay put until the crisis was over. Things cooled down a little over the weekend, and President Johnson declared Sunday a national day of mourning. The office was closed out of respect (and also out of fear of riots) on

Monday and Tuesday, extending our period of mourning along with the rest of the nation's.

On Tuesday, April 9, thousands and thousands of people lined the streets. A mule-drawn wagon, much like the one that drove the slaves back and forth to the fields of Retreat Plantation on St. Simons Island, carried Martin Luther King Jr.'s casket to Ebenezer Baptist Church. It was a heartbreaking sight, even on television. Later in the week when things had settled down, offices opened again, and life for us got back to normal. Two months later the news came out that James Earl Ray, a white man, had been captured at London Heathrow Airport. He was charged with the assassination of Martin Luther King Jr. It just made you shake your head and ask why.

That summer I took my vacation and went to see my family at St. Simons. I hopped into my little Camaro with Todd and Gayle, and off we went. It was so exciting to go and visit my mother where we could talk without the pressures that Raymond caused. But when it came to my father, our relationship was very strained. Because the memories of the past were still haunting me, I was very cool with Daddy. Mother soon saw how happy I was since leaving Raymond. I was a young woman in love with life, and my children were so sweet and well behaved. They were such a joy, and I thanked God every day for giving them to me.

Shortly after, we were all shaken by the news that Bobby Kennedy, brother to President Kennedy, had been shot in Los Angeles, California, at the Ambassador Hotel by a Palestinian immigrant named Sirhan Sirhan. Kennedy had been shot three times and died twenty-seven hours later. Like my mother, I was beginning to hate politics. If all our best people were subjected to assassinations, who would ever want to be a leader or representative of people? What in the world was going to happen next?

Roger and his roommate Jack owned a 1946 Taylorcraft airplane. Roger and I made plans for him to fly to St. Simons in late summer and pick me up at the Malcolm McKinnon Airport. He was going to fly me to his aunt and uncle's farm in Cuthbert so that his parents and I could meet. The flight was fine, but we had a bumpy landing in his uncle's peanut field. I put my life in Roger's hands and survived the landing. Now I had to survive meeting his parents. I had never been more nervous in my life.

I could see Roger's mother was visibly shaken over the fact that I was divorced and had two children. She just couldn't see her son as a grown man. He was the center of their life and a product of their achievement in raising a child. They hadn't planned on Roger getting involved with a divorcée and her children. In some ways, deep inside, I too felt he could have done much better.

After the vacation I wasn't really sure where I stood with his family, but Roger and I continued to date and work as usual. I painted every spare minute to get ready for my art show, which was coming up in December. At Thanksgiving, I went to my parents' in St. Simons, and Roger went to his in Valdosta. As soon as I returned, I was busy finishing my paintings and framing my artwork for the December show.

My second collection looked totally different from the naive art I had shown the previous December. The visual imagery was probably from my subconscious, for it had a surreal quality to it. I was no longer in the blue period. My paintings were softer in color and paid greater attention to perspective. I painted landscapes, portraits of black children in choir gowns, and one large portrait of a clown in patriotic colors.

On Monday morning, December 2, 1968, I drove to the National Bank of Georgia on West Peachtree Street to hang my show. The bank had a black doorman named John, and he wasn't a very friendly man. You'd think that he was a royal guardsman at the Tower of London; he was so stern, put on airs, and never smiled.

I struggled back and forth to my car carrying my paintings, and John stood there offering no assistance. When I started bringing in the group of choir girl portraits though, you should have seen the look of shock on his face. He lost all of his composure, jumped up and down, and began yelling, "Black is beautiful! Black is beautiful!" I quickly hushed him. Now he was there to assist me in every way—even holding the ladder and handing me paintings as I hung the show. John told me that of all the artists who had done shows there over the years, no one had ever depicted black people.

I rushed to my office exhausted, grabbed a quick cup of coffee, and started working. Just after lunch, Mr. Tyre, my boss, came over to me and explained that there was a problem with my art at the bank.

"What? You're kidding me," I responded in shock.

He excused me and told me to go clear up the problem. I was so disappointed. Was the problem with the white customers or the black customers? A huge part of the exhibit consisted of portraits of the choir girls.

When I got to the bank, I slowly walked into the president's office. He greeted me with "Carol, we have had some great responses thus far from our customers. However, the painting of the clown looks too much like President Johnson, and we need you to take it down." I burst out laughing, and he did too. I took it back to the office to show it to everyone. I must admit that it really did look like LBJ. He was a very unpopular president at that time because of the Vietnam War. He had contributed to the increase in troops and caused the war to be prolonged.

On August 2, 1964, the North Vietnamese fired directly on two US ships sitting in international waters at the Gulf of Tonkin. Congress responded by passing the Gulf of Tonkin Resolution, which gave President Johnson the authority to escalate US involvement in Vietnam. Hundreds of thousands of US troops were sent in. It would prove to be a no-win war leaving the United States with around fifty-eight thousand fatalities. Having a good laugh at LBJ made everyone feel good.

At the end of the month, I had another sold-out show. Also, I was shocked to get an invitation, because of John, to show my art at Spelman College in Atlanta. America's oldest college for black women was founded in 1881 by two female teachers and a Baptist minister in the basement of Friendship Baptist Church. Sadly, I was too frightened to show my work there as a white woman because of the racial unrest. John understood. From then on John greeted me with a smile and graciously opened the door for me.

Roger had gone home to Valdosta for Christmas, and he stayed over through New Year's. I was a little sad about that but happy to see him when he returned. I could tell something was bothering him the minute that I saw him. He sat me down and told me he had something important to discuss with me. Oh no! I just knew he was going to break up with me, and I could feel my tears welling up. Roger looked me straight in my eyes, and then out it came.

"We are getting married."

"We are?"

"Yes, for the children's sake. I love you."

At first I started laughing, and then it turned to crying.

"I have a plan. Let me know if you like it," he said. "I've given my notice at work, and after I finish we'll get married. No one will be invited to the wedding except the children and maybe a witness."

"Why? Is it because of your family?"

Roger looked at me. "This is the plan. Do you like it? Yes or no?"

Of course, I said yes.

Roger worked out his notice, and we were married in late January in a very private ceremony at the First Methodist Church in Austell by Reverend Maxwell. He was the pastor who had previously written the letter to me while Raymond and I were separated. We had a very small reception at my apartment, where Roger and I were going to be living with the children.

From January to March, Roger worked as a senate reading clerk for the Georgia General Assembly. He loved his job and enjoyed learning a lot from the secretary of the senate, Hamilton McWhorter. Roger and I were invited to many parties and events as part of his position.

After the senate convened, Roger got a job selling carpets at night. During the day, I continued to work, and he stayed home with the children while studying for the bar exam that was coming up in July. He studied very hard, but unfortunately he didn't pass the exam. He was devastated. Roger had never failed an exam in his life, and I guess he had just spread himself too thin. I felt so guilty that the children and I had taken him away from his studies. The next go-around would be different.

In February 1970, Roger took the bar exam and passed. He continued his work as reading clerk in the senate that year. After the senate recessed, he found a job in Marietta at a successful law firm. He was happy as a clam. We could see a bright future ahead for us. He had only worked there for about six months when we got the news that Roger's father, Dorsey, had terminal prostate cancer. His mother needed his support and wanted him back home. We quickly packed up and headed south to Valdosta.

With the help of his parents, Roger and I bought a small, white-framed house on the water at Twin Lakes. I enrolled the children in school, and Roger found a job at a local law firm. We settled into our home, and soon I got involved in set design at the Little Theatre and joined the Town and Country Garden Club. Under the mentorship of a very fine Valdosta matriarch, I worked my way to being president of the club, and I became cochair and chairperson of the antique show. Roger reconnected with some of his old schoolmates, and we made lots of new friends. We didn't have a lot of money, but we were very happy with our new life together.

It was a very sad time when Roger's father passed away. His mother was extremely dependent on Roger. I was understanding during this time of great loss (after all, he was her only child), but it would get worse—so much so that Roger wasn't coming home to us but going to her house for lunch, and if working late, he'd go have dinner with her too. A friend of mine suggested that we join him at his mother's, believing that she would either stop asking him to come for so many meals or would love having us join them. Well, it worked. We were there every meal, and Mary grew to love the children. We ended up having a great relationship.

Then I became pregnant. Everyone was so excited. Roger's mother was over the moon with excitement. The pregnancy went well, and Judy, my friend and neighbor, gave me a lovely baby shower. I prepared the nursery in great anticipation of this baby. This child would bring all the members of our family together in a way that they hadn't—and perhaps couldn't - bond before. I hadn't come to full term, when I was taken to the hospital for an emergency delivery. On September 1, 1971, Conrad Earl Douglas was born. The next thing I knew, Roger was standing at my bedside.

"Carol, the baby has died. It was a boy."

"What? Where's my baby? What happened?"

"He couldn't breathe. He had hyaline membrane disease."

I was somewhat knowledgeable about this disease. I knew that Jacqueline Kennedy had lost a son to this same disease in August 1963.

"I want to see him!"

"Honey, Mother and I decided it would be best if you didn't see him."

"I want to see him! I need to see my baby."

"Carol, the mortician has already picked him up. It's too late." Roger drew a Polaroid snapshot out of his pocket. "The nurse took this photo of him. Here's our son."

"Oh Roger, he was so beautiful!"

He later came to regret showing me the photo. They immediately had to sedate me. I just couldn't believe what had happened.

Going home with my arms empty after giving birth to a beloved child we'd already accepted as a full-fledged member of the family was devastating. Todd and Gayle were very sad and upset to lose their baby brother.

No one had expected this to happen, and the empty nursery was a daily reminder of our child who never came home—our dream that came to life and was crushed by a terrible, horridly unfair disease.

The Valium only worked for a week. I was in a total stupor, and I had to pull myself together for the sake of my family. Roger, who had just lost his father and now his child, became very distant. I felt so sad for him, and I believed that somehow I had failed him. Neither one of us shared our grief with the other. Instead of filling the fissure of grief with our tears and forming a bridge with grasped hands, each of us retreated into our own cocoon of shame and hurt, and the gaping wound between us grew into an abysmal chasm.

Time passed in a slow haze just as ticks of the clock and squares on the calendar offer blind routines that get you through days, weeks, and months. Roger and another lawyer named Lamar opened a new law firm on the main square of Valdosta. He threw himself totally into the work of his law practice. Civic activities and garden club work no longer challenged me or gave me any pleasure, so I'd come home feeling bored and depressed. Trying to stay busy, I would often go to work for Lamar, the state court solicitor. I'd do state court warrants and other small jobs.

Roger and I joined Francis Lake Golf Club. He thought it might help me get over my sadness about losing the baby and give me a new activity that would be healthy and outdoors. Only once did Roger and I play nine holes together. That was all he ever played with me. Instead, he had purchased a motorcycle for dirt bike racing. When he had spare time, he spent it racing with some most undesirable people. I wanted nothing to do with them.

I soon became a very good golfer with the help of Dynamite Goodloe. He was acclaimed as one of the best and most colorful golfers in the country. He had an outstanding amateur golf record. Dynamite was the epitome of a gentleman on the golf course. We were often paired together and had some brilliant rounds of golf. His instructions became one of the greatest gifts I ever received.

Roger had always wanted to own his own plane, so later that year, we bought a Cessna 172. We took trips to Key West, Bimini, and many other places. On occasion, Roger would get motion sickness, and I would have to take over the controls. He thought it would be a good idea for me to take flying lessons. I was certainly interested in starting lessons, but then I received an urgent call from my mother on February 10, 1976. My father had suffered another stroke. She asked me to please come and help her care for him along with my sisters Betty and Vera and my sister-in-law Patsy. Mother was adamant about not putting him in a nursing home. I left my husband and two children in Valdosta and arrived at St. Simons to find my mother totally exhausted.

Mother had set up a hospital bed in the living room so that Daddy would have our full attention. He proved to be a most demanding patient. This stroke had left him paralyzed on the right side, and so he was unable to walk or feed himself. His speech being slurred, he grunted out commands and grew frustrated when we didn't understand. I was only there a few days when he had another stroke and had to be hospitalized. We all insisted that Mother stay home and rest while the four of us took shifts caring for Daddy.

One night when I took the night shift at the hospital, I slept in a chair near his bed. I started hearing grunts, so I got up and walked over to his bed.

"Daddy, what do you want? Bathroom? Pee? I'll get the attendant." He grunted and shook his head. His cold blue eyes pierced into me.

"Water?"

Again, he vigorously shook his head no and stared at me with the same piercing look. He put two fingers to his lips.

"Oh, you want a cigarette. Daddy, I'm sorry, but you can't smoke in the hospital. It's not allowed. Are you cold?"

I comforted him with a blanket. He shook with anger and kept staring at me with that same look that had always put the fear of God into me.

I went back over to the chair, sat back down, and stretched out. I was sitting there dozing when suddenly I felt a warm sensation on my cheek. I touched my face; it was wet. I smelled it. It smelled awful! My eyes popped open, and I looked at Daddy. He was urinating on me! I jumped up from my chair and went over to his bedside. I looked him straight in the eyes, and a voice came out of me that shocked me with its raw emotion.

"You son of a bitch! You have shit on me all my life, and now you're pissing on me! You son of a bitch!"

I burst into tears and ran out of the room into the hallway. Leaning against the wall, I slid down to the floor sobbing. I mean sobbing hysterically. A male nurse came running down the hall. He dropped to his knees and asked, "Has your father died?" I looked up at him with tears running down my face and explained that no, he wasn't dead; he had just peed on me.

"I hate that son of a bitch! I hate him! I hate him!"

This nurse was black and had two gold crowns on his front teeth with a star in one of them. I remember staring at it with a fixed gaze as he spoke to me. He helped me to my feet and held me up, holding me in his arms.

"Now, now, stop crying." He was so gentle and sweet. Finally, I stopped sobbing. He stood back and took my face into his hands, looked straight into my eyes, and said, "I don't want you coming back to this hospital to see him again."

"OK." I nodded.

"Now you go home."

I nodded again. "OK."

Driving home across the causeway, I tried to stay in control of my car as headlights of the oncoming cars blinded me. I wished that someone would drive into me head-on and just take me out of my misery.

Arriving home, I walked slowly along the sidewalk, praying that Mother wouldn't be awake. I wanted to shower and wash the urine out of my hair and off of my face before she woke. That old feeling of numbness was in my head. If only shampoo, soap, and water could wash away the memory of what had just happened. No water was hot enough to cleanse me of the years of fear and insult. No soap could dissolve the grime of Daddy's last act toward me.

After bathing, I wrapped a towel around my chilled body. I dashed out of the bathroom into the night's cool air on the porch and through the kitchen to my old bedroom. Angrily throwing the towel across the room, I quickly put on my nightclothes and got into bed. I pulled the covers over my face, ready to muffle any sound that would bellow from the depths of my hysteria. But no sound came. It just didn't happen. I lay there staring at the faint light that peeked through the covers. "Cry, you fool! Cry! Let it out!" It wouldn't come. "Cry! Cry! Cry!" I was so full of anger that I just kept thinking, "You SOB. You SOB." I finally fell into a deep sleep, and when I awoke, it was morning.

"OK, tiger," I thought, "time for a new day." Acting like nothing had happened, I sat and had breakfast with my mother, trying to be upbeat. I made no mention of what Daddy had done to me last night.

That morning I decided I would stay at home and take care of Mother. I would let the others care for Daddy. It was only a few days later when Betty called from the hospital to say that Daddy had suffered a massive stroke and died.

I started crying. It wasn't grief over the loss of my daddy so much as it was grief over the loss of what could have and should have been. A one-sided dialogue with my dead father began in my thoughts.

"I'm hurt and angry with you, Daddy. I'm not just angry about what you did to me but what you did to each and every one of us. Your actions impacted everyone I loved. Their pain is my pain. I just pray to God that I can forgive you someday! Until then, for the rage, disgust, and hatred that I hold toward you, God have mercy on my soul."

Mother was devastated. She collapsed and was put to bed. We were all very concerned about her health; she was very pale, short of breath, and exhausted. She seemed unprepared to cope with the situation. I couldn't help but think about how it would be awful if, after all Mother had gone through, she didn't make it. She overcame so many battles with my father and his disease, and now there was the possibility of losing the war.

Soon she gained enough strength to make funeral arrangements. Eliza, our dear friend from my earliest childhood, came to comfort her and helped out in many ways. Mother needed Eliza now more than ever. Our little house was soon overflowing with many friends and relatives. My father was the eldest of twelve children, and my mother one of ten children. I had thirty-eight aunts and uncles and fifty-two first cousins. I didn't know all of their names. Day and night they filled the house. The women mostly gravitated toward the kitchen and living room; the men stood on the front porch or sat around the table on the patio in the backyard.

This gathering of people eventually took on the spirit of a party. Everyone was talking about my father's abilities, achievements, and escapades. It was a celebration of a very complex man. I couldn't tell you exactly how I was feeling. Maybe it was the condition I call numbness—that feeling I'd get after a horrible incident with Daddy that left my brain numb, frozen, unable to translate thoughts, and without reasoning power or emotion. Lost in time.

Our family had many friends who also came to pay their respects. I was sitting in the living room chatting with some of my relatives when I heard a loud knock at the front door. I opened it, and there stood a black couple. They asked, "Is Mrs. Hamby home? We would like to see her."

I said, "Yes, just a minute," as I left them standing at the door.

I ran into the kitchen where Mother was sitting and said, "Mother, there are some black people at the front door."

"Child, what's wrong with you? Don't leave them standing on the porch. Invite them in."

I went back to the door and invited them in, taking them to the kitchen. They gave my mother a hug, and she asked them to sit down at the table with her. She poured them a cup of hot coffee and gave them a slice of cake.

The woman started talking about how, through the years, when they were down on their luck, sure enough "Mr. Coon Bill" would bring them some fish or hog meat.

"He was a good man, Mrs. Hamby," the husband said. "He did lots of nice things for the black folks." They continued talking about Daddy as tears ran down their faces. Now everyone at the table was crying, including me. This was such a pure expression of human emotion, like nothing I had seen in the past few days. What a wonderful thing my daddy had done for these people. How could this be the same person? I felt very perplexed.

"I remember riding with Daddy in the truck," I chipped in. "We dropped off fish at different families' houses on the north end of the island, at Jewtown and on Proctor Lane. Yeah, he had lots of black friends."

The next day we had a graveside service at Frederica Gardens. There were many cars parked along the roadway. We somberly walked to a tent where chairs were set up for our family. We took our seats as six pallbearers carried the casket with two honorary pallbearers following. The casket was placed in its appropriate place, and all of the pallbearers stood flanking it. It was a somber moment.

Then, Mother got a hard poke in her back. She quickly turned and asked, "What?"

My uncle leaned over and whispered, "What are those two black guys doing there?"

"They are honorary pallbearers. Bill requested that they be pallbearers, but we decided the strong, young nephews should carry the casket." In a short manner, she told my uncle that these men were two of my father's best friends—Connie Jackson and Levy Davis. "Do you have a problem with that?"

My uncle snapped back, "No. I don't."

I thought, "Maybe you didn't know your brother as well as you thought you did." From what I knew of my daddy, with all of his awful behaviors, I swore there was not a prejudiced bone in his body.

Just after the funeral, Jean Holliman, a friend and nurse whom Mother had worked with in the Brunswick hospital many years ago, asked Mother if she was going to be OK financially. Jean apologized for asking, saying she did it out of concern for Mother.

"Bill didn't have any life insurance," Mother admitted, "and there's nothing left in our savings."

"Grace, after things settle down, I'll help you get a nursing job on Sea Island. You will have to take a course or two, but you will be fine."

Within weeks Mother was working on Sea Island and making very good wages. She saved money and became independent. She even went on a cruise, bought a new car, bought new clothes, and started wearing makeup and having her hair done regularly. She blossomed.

Her first patient was a lovely lady whom she went on to take care of for many years. After the lady's death, Mother stayed to be a companion to the lady's husband, a retired president of AT&T. Over time they developed a wonderful relationship. He did ask her to marry him, but she refused. We couldn't believe it!

"Mother, he's perfect," I said. "I distinctly remember you telling us once that you wanted to find a rich man with one foot in the grave and the other on a banana peel."

"Oh, Carol, I never said that!" I just laughed. She told me that she never wanted to lose her independence again. She was happy with her life as it was, even though she cared about this man. He passed away shortly after that.

Mother worked for fifteen years. The last two years of her life, she started having ministrokes and had to retire. She had accumulated a large amount of money, which gave her security and independence and allowed her to avoid being a burden to anyone.

For many years, I thought that Mother was weak because she stayed with my father. How many times had we packed up the car to finally leave him and she had changed her mind and decided to stay? She always forgave him. Now, for the first time, I saw her differently. Mother was not a weak woman at all. She had found strength, through her Christian faith, to keep on going. That was what carried her through all of those hard years. My mother had walked the path of grace.

It was in March 1976 that I started taking flying lessons. I had already experienced flying with Roger in his old Taylorcraft, and I had copiloted in our Cessna. But this was the first time I actually flew the plane myself. I found it to be a most thrilling experience, and my instructor, after our first lesson, said I was a natural at flying. I took my first solo flight on May 24, after completing just short of ten instruction hours.

Roger was so proud of me. As I exited the plane after my solo flight, one of the pilots at the airport cut off the tail of my shirt, an initiation for soloing. He then put an old aviator cap on my head and a yellow silk scarf around my neck and asked me to slip on a blue flight suit. Pulling out his camera, he told me to look serious, and then he took my picture.

"You look just like Amelia Earhart," he said.

"Well, all I can say is that this scarf you wrapped around my neck perfectly matches the yellow stripe down my back!"

"I don't think so, Carol," he said, laughing. "Do you know how few women solo under ten hours?" I had no idea, but I knew how much I admired Amelia Earhart, the first woman to fly solo across the Atlantic. She was one of my childhood heroines.

A few days went by before I received the photo. I broke out in laughter. Well, I certainly wasn't an Amelia Earhart, but I could pretend, couldn't I?

I went to the doctor, who was an acquaintance of the family, to get my flight physical, and he made a comment to me about the dangers of flying.

"Who cares if I live or die?" I responded flippantly. He stopped me right there.

"What will happen to your children if something happens to you?" His question felt like a slap in the face. I wasn't taking chances with my own life and future; I was being reckless with theirs!

I passed my physical and started to get my pilot's license, all in record time. No longer the girl from the wrong side of the tracks or the divorcée who might be an easy victory for some young man, I was doing something many men couldn't do and very few women had. This was something to be proud of.

Despite my achievement, the doctor's comment kept echoing in my head, and I had to admit I was uncomfortable because it rang true. What was really important here? If I sought thrills that appeased the pain and humiliation of others' measurements of me, what did that say about my values? It didn't matter which side of the tracks I came from. I had to live with myself and judge my own actions. I realized that I needed to think about my children and their welfare first.

And so I stopped flying. My wings were clipped.

It was in August that things went downhill in my relationship with Roger. He went one direction and I another. Unfortunately, it wasn't a pretty sight on both of our parts. I just didn't care anymore. I had failed to give him a child, but his decisions had put such a burden on me that I couldn't live with myself or with him feeling that he no longer loved me. I certainly wasn't going to stay in a loveless marriage.

We agreed that our marriage was over. I met Roger at his law office, where we signed the divorce papers. I packed my bags and took my children to St. Simons. I knew that I would be in good hands with my mother. I had tons of emotional baggage, but if anything could give me the strength to carry on, it would be Mother and my faith in God.

Roger E. Douglas
Attorney at Law
North Ashley Street
Valdosta, Georgia 31601

Ms. Carol J. Douglas
Valdosta, Georgia 31601

October 20, 1976

Here are a few things I want to say to you before we finally terminate our marriage. First I would like to make it clear that I have always loved you. In fact I love you now as much or even in spite of what happened. You may not believe this but it is the truth. You have said many times that I knew you would leave me and I was preparing for it but I was willing to live with you forever. I have never wanted you to go and never thought you would. If you are leaving me because I don't love you, you are mistaken. If you're leaving because you don't love me anymore I understand.

I knew you were severely hurt and for that I am truly sorry, but no one can change the past. The decisions I made appeared easy for me especially when you bore the burden. Had I known what I know now I never would have made them.

I have always been extremely proud of you. I may not have expressed it as I should have but I felt it very deeply.

It may sound strange, but if you ever need help I will be available. I just can't see knowing someone intimately for nine years and then turning off all feelings as if to turn off a faucet.

It is not easy for me to write this. I hope you will accept this letter as an expression of my true feelings toward you. I blame myself for what has happened. All I can say is that I love you very much and I wish you well.

Roger

Our divorce was final in November 1976. Now I had to move on and start building a new life.

Chapter 29

BOB

It was October, and I had been staying with Mother for only a few weeks when I decided to rent a furnished house on the beach. Mother was quite protective of me, and she would not let anyone from Valdosta communicate with me. She knew I needed time alone without any interference. That was partly why I was surprised when she suggested that I go to meet our new pastor, Felix Haynes, at the First Baptist Church of St. Simons. She was aware that what I really needed was spiritual guidance. Nearing December, she said I should go with my sister-in-law, Patsy.

"No! I'm not going with her. She sits down with all of the children in the front row. She raises her hands and sways and does all of those hallelujahs and amens." Then Mother gave me the look.

"You are going, Carol. Even if you sit in the back row. Just go."

"OK. I'll be a good girl and go."

The next Sunday Patsy picked me up at Mother's, and the children stayed behind to visit with their grandmother. Off we rushed to the church. When we entered the door, Patsy hurried down to the front, but I looked around the back of the church, trying to find a spot where no one was sitting. The pew in the far back corner of the church was perfect. I found just the right seat and settled in. The pews were empty in front and back of me.

I was only seated for a few minutes when a man entered the other end of my pew. He was holding a lady by the hand. They edged along the pew getting closer and closer to me. What? With all of these pews is he choosing this one? Soon the gentleman was about to sit down inches from me. Damn!

As he started to sit down, I touched him on the elbow. He looked sharply at me.

"I'm sorry, sir, but you can't sit here. You'd better choose another seat."

"Why?" he asked.

Feeling self-conscious, I looked at him and said, "Sir, this pew is reserved for sinners." A big smile came across his face, and then he turned to the lady.

"Sit down, honey. We have the right pew."

I recognized the lady as someone I had worked with at SeaPak. Her name was Cora. She introduced him as her friend, Al, who was visiting from Canada. They sat down, and we chuckled together. We were soon hushed by others sitting near us as the church service began. As we quieted, I began to reflect on my life. Mother was right; I needed to go to church. I did need God. I was at an all-time low in my life. It was time to stop wallowing in my misery. Turning to God, I knew that he'd give me the strength to carry on. He was my rock.

We drove home to Mother's and enjoyed a lovely Sunday dinner that she had prepared.

"Carol, don't you feel better now that you've gone to church?" Mother asked.

"Yes, Mother, I do. I asked the Lord for strength and forgiveness." Then I told her that I had also asked him to bring me a new husband. I giggled.

"That's OK. The Lord will answer your prayers."

It was on Monday that my mother received a call from Cora and Al. They wanted me to have dinner with them and meet a friend of theirs. When Mother told me this, I quickly said no.

"Why not? It's a sin to wallow in your misery."

"Mother, this is a blind date! I had one in high school that I've always tried to forget. The boy had a severe case of acne, and his face was covered with tiny volcanoes ready to erupt at any time. No blind date!"

"This man is too old to have acne. You are going!"

And so it was that evening that I met Bob, a tall, well-dressed, and very distinguished-looking man. My heart just fluttered. We had a wonderful time that night at dinner, and he asked me to join him for lunch the next day before he left for Canada. Bob was the senior partner at Touche-Ross, an international accounting firm in Kitchener, Ontario.

We started dating, and from that day forward, we never looked back. They say that distance makes the heart grow fonder, but at times it makes the heart grow weary, and our long-distance relationship had its difficulties. No sooner than we got together did it seem Bob was flying back to Canada. It was like having a fascinating conversation amid constant interruptions, and the spaces between sentences seemed interminably long. I now worked as a dental receptionist at Dr. John Hendry's office at The Pier. Between this job and caring for the children, time went by a little more easily. We continued our relationship for about a year, and then Bob asked me to marry him and move to Canada. Mother was right. The Lord had answered my prayers.

Our wedding day.

On December 27, 1979, we were married at the Island Club on St. Simons. We had a stunning wedding, and I had a couturier wedding dress. A fabulous floral designer did our flowers and the Cloister made our beautiful wedding cake. Even though I had been married twice before, Bob wanted this to be a memorable, very special moment. Bob's children, Karen and Sean, flew down from Canada with their grandparents. Karen was sixteen— a lovely young woman with dark-brown hair and just full of personality. Sean was only thirteen, and he was much more emotional about his father marrying me. By now Bob's children and my children had become close friends, and we ended up having a lovely celebration of our marriage.

The Best of Both Worlds

I was leaving this beautiful paradise to go live in a country that was worlds apart from what I was accustomed to. I was confident that Bob and I would have a good marriage and wonderful life together, and it would be the best move for my children.

We kept my house, which I had recently built on Peachtree Street. In Canada, we rented a high-rise penthouse apartment. I found apartment living difficult and got a little homesick, so I bought an existing business to have something to keep me busy until I adjusted to my new life. It was a bath boutique called A Touch of Class.

Soon after that, we purchased a lovely home just a few houses from Westmount Golf Club. I started playing golf again, made a lot of new friends, and really enjoyed the social life. Southerners certainly don't have anything over Canadians when it comes to hospitality.

My daughter Gayle was fourteen, and I enrolled her in the ninth grade, where she was excited to take French. Unfortunately, Todd, now sixteen, wanted to go and live with his father in Acworth, Georgia. That only lasted about five months. One day Mother found Todd knocking at her front door, and he asked if he could live with her. Mother was in shock. Todd explained that he no longer wanted to live with his father.

"Todd, you are welcome to stay as long as you please. No one is going to force you to live with your father." So Todd stayed and lived with Mother until he graduated.

Bob and I purchased a ski chalet near Collingwood, Ontario. On the weekends all the kids would come and enjoy skiing with us. It was one of the best things that we had ever done for our kids. We became a very close family.

It took me a while to learn to ski. I hated it at first and wanted to quit until my friend Trudy told me what might happen to me.

"First you'll start wearing warm-up suits, then you'll get fat and do nothing but household chores, and finally you'll get cabin fever and go mad!"

I was quickly hitting the slopes and learned to really love skiing. I became particularly good at après-skiing, which is French for *after-skiing*—going out, having drinks, dancing, and generally having fun after a day on the snow.

I also became famous with my friends for my cookies. These oatmeal cookies were chock-full of pecans and raisins, brown sugar, and cinnamon. When one was tossed through the air and hit the table, it would usually bounce at least three times. Once my friend, Bill, picked one up and said, "This is not a cookie. It's a hockey puck." My friends laughed, but you'd better believe that when I'd arrive with my tin of cookies, every single one of them would say, "I want one of your hockey pucks, Carol!"

Bob soon left Touché-Ross to go into the hotel business full-time with some Canadian investors. The majority of the hotels were Holiday Inns located in the southeastern United States. The company did well enough to buy an airplane. Bob made monthly trips to Savannah, where he had an office with his partner, Roger. I'd fly down with him, making regular visits to my family.

On August 15, 1982, my sister Betty died from cancer. She had still claimed me as her baby. She'd always say, "You know that Mother gave you to me when you were born and brought you home from the hospital." I hated seeing her suffer all of those months. She was a loving and wonderful sister, and it broke my heart to see her go.

Bob and I started traveling a lot with some of our skiing friends. We went to Europe, where I delighted in learning about the cultures of different countries. We also made trips to Colorado, sometimes taking the children.

As members of the International Association of Holiday Inns, we went on many fabulous trips every year. The Holiday Inn conferences brought us to many cities in the United States and to England once. We were not holidaying all of the time, because Bob and his partner worked many hours to make the hotels a success. I was recruited, along with Roger's wife, Deborah, to help in a number of ways. We chose the decor for the different hotels and entertained the partners. Deborah was a hard worker and contributed wholeheartedly. It was a wonderful, exciting time.

Bob and I then embarked upon one of our more interesting ventures. Along with other investors, we bought Ratz-Bechtel Funeral Home in Kitchener. Originally built as the Kaufman mansion, it was elaborate in every detail. I was asked by the partners to redecorate the facility, and so I had the opportunity to get to know the wonderful members of the staff. They were some of the most optimistic people that I had ever worked with.

Bob and his partners by now owned more than a dozen hotels, and he was spending more time in Georgia with the management company. I took advantage of his trips in the company's plane to go south and spend more time with my mother and family. My mother's health was now in decline. She had had several ministrokes but had recovered quite well from them.

While visiting her in Georgia, I would ask her if she wanted to go to the Cloister Hotel for lunch. She would decline me every time, saying, "No. Just take me to Brunswick to Willie's Wee-Nee Wagon." I would take her, and there she would sit in the car eating her pork-chop sandwich. Willie, the proprietor, would come out to the car and have a little chat with her. It made her feel like a million dollars.

One day while Mother was shopping in the grocery store, she ran into Eliza, who asked her to arrange a visit with me. Mother said, "OK, and I'll even bake you your favorite chocolate cake." Later Mother called me, and we made plans to get together.

Eliza was a very special person to me. I loved her sparkly eyes and her sweet face. When I was a child, she would take my hand first in a tentative way and then pull me closer and closer like she was testing me one inch at a time to see if I was receptive. Then she would grab me and squeeze me, laughing and saying, "You sweet baby child, my sweet baby Carol Jane." This was followed by hugs, kisses, and laughter. It tickled me to death.

These days Eliza would occasionally come and help my mother catch up on her housework, but Mother needed her more as a friend. They would sit at the kitchen table sipping coffee and having heart-to-heart talks for hours.

Eliza did marry a man named Pete Harrison, but they never had children. They lived in a little house on Proctor Lane with her mother. Over the years, my family members would drop off fish or stop for a quick visit with them.

When Betty passed away, Eliza and Pete came by to pay their respects. It was a very emotional visit for Eliza. She was especially overcome with grief. She had been drinking, but we took no offense. I don't think that it was the alcohol bringing on the tears but more the love that she felt for Betty and the sadness of our family's grief. It was about this time that I noticed Eliza's drinking had become a very serious problem. Within a couple of blocks of their home were a number of juke joints. The LaQuartz Club, the Blue Inn Club, the 400 Club, Shoe Shop Joe's, Hazel's Cafe, and others were within walking distance of one another. The LaQuartz Club and the Blue Inn Club were very popular spots. Entertainers like Louis Armstrong, Arthur Prysock, Buddy Johnson and his orchestra, Ella Johnson, Eddie "Guitar Slim" Jones, and many others performed there. All of these bars were hangouts for the local folk. Many times I would see Eliza and Pete standing outside these joints and give them a quick wave.

Pete later died, and Eliza moved in to a little yellow house that looked like a dollhouse. She wanted to be near her sister Louise, whom she depended on for most everything for the rest of her life. Louise was a fine lady. She worked many years on Sea Island and was respected by all.

It was only a few months later that we all got together.

"Now, Miss Baby Carol Jane, tell me all about living in Canada."

"Well, Eliza, it gets so cold up there it could literally freeze your tits off." She shrieked with laughter.

"I can go into the grocery store to shop, and when I come back out to the car, it will be covered with snow. I have to take this little broom and sweep the snow off the windshield, hood, and side and back windows. Even my headlights and taillights need to be swept. By now my hands and feet are frozen, and there's an inch of snow on top of my head and snow on my eyelashes, which makes my mascara run down my face. By now, I'm pissed off, Eliza." There were more shrieks of laughter, and tears rolled down her cheeks.

"When I finally get back into the car, I have to drive straight home because my groceries will freeze if they're left in the car, even if just for a few minutes. And I feel as cold as those nearly frozen groceries. It seems like the car's heater was designed to warm up just as you arrive home and pull into the garage."

Eliza's eyes were the size of saucers.

"Now, Missy Carol, it ain't right you living up there!" She looked at Mother for approval. "Ain't natural, Miz Hamby; it's like taking an alligator out of the Okefenokee and throwing him in the snow. You think he's goin' to like it? No! No! He ain't goin' to like that. It's just ain't natural." She looked at me. "You don't like it up there, do you? You gone and made a deal with the devil when you married dat man!" Mother and I burst into laughter. With great excitement, Eliza said, "You were born here on this island, and dat's where you need to stay." Trying to distract Eliza from getting overwrought, Mother quickly jumped up from the table and served us coffee and cake. It was the only thing that would calm Eliza down about the deal I had made with the devil. It was an amazing visit. We all laughed until we cried. Eliza was such a funny person. Over the years I would arrange these visits to share my life stories with her.

"Eliza, I have just been to Africa. I wish you could have been with me. The people are beautiful. I was afraid to speak because their English was much better than mine." I showed her pictures from my trip and from our safari. I told her about seeing all of the major African animals. An elephant even chased after us one day while we were out on safari. Once a baby hippo ran alongside our jeep until its mother caught up to it and herded it away. So many exciting things happened on our safari.

We went to Soweto and visited Winnie Mandela's home. It had become a shrine to Nelson Mandela. I saw lots of his personal papers and keepsakes. Our guide gave us a tour of the shantytown in Soweto, where there were hundreds of shacks made of scraps of wood and tin. They didn't have running water and used a communal toilet. People told us not to go there because it was so dangerous. We went any way because we wanted to see the real Africa. Even though they lived in horrific conditions, they still seemed to be happy and treated us kindly. Eliza was in total awe.

We also saw Victoria Falls and Zambezi River. Our most favorite part of the trip was visiting a children's primary school in the bush, forty kilometers from Victoria Falls. These were the most well-behaved and most beautiful children I think I have ever seen. Later we visited a village where they invited us inside a thatch hut and shared their food with us.

"I loved Africa, Eliza, but St. Simons Island is a much better place for you to live in my opinion." She smiled and agreed.

"Not bad, Eliza, for a poor, snotty-nosed little girl from St. Simons Island to get to see the world."

The Bump in the Road

It was in May 1989 that Bob's and my marriage hit a bump in the road. We were both equally mad at each other. Our marriage got off track over a personal and business situation that got totally out of control. We were legally separated for a couple of months.

This time I searched out a psychologist to help me through this crisis. She said that my tendency was to run away when I got hurt by someone I loved. This stemmed from wanting my mother to leave my daddy.

"You can't keep running," she said. "Don't let the image of who your father was distort that of Bob. When you do, your father controls your life. Carol, you have to face your problems and work through them together. Once you give it a good attempt, if you feel it is too much for you, then go ahead and leave. No one is going to force you to stay in a loveless relationship. But if you run away before trying, you'll always wonder if you made the right choice."

It wasn't until Bob handed me this letter to read that I realized how much he loved me.

July 27, 1989
Dear Carol,

This is a love letter! I know—it's been a long time. September 1978 to be exact. The last one I wrote was in Fiji, and I hand delivered it to you, as I am now. This won't be a long one for it's easy for me to say that I love you more than anyone or anything on _earth_ and always will.

I pray that, through the help of God, we can have a long and lasting love and friendship, and we can overcome any and all obstacles to our relationship. You can be assured that I will do everything in my power to ensure this.

I'll need help, and I hope that through prayer and by putting Christ in the centre of my life that this desire can be accomplished.

You are a beautiful, warm, and vivacious person, a wonderful companion and loving wife, and I thank God for the opportunity to renew our marriage.
All my love,
Bob

I burst into tears.

With my counselor's guidance and my pastor's support, we resolved our problems. I know that people don't believe it, but our love grew greater than before. Thank God we were able to put our anger to rest and renew our love for each other.

Bob and I enjoyed many special moments with his father and mother, Frank and Vera, and his sister Barbara and her family. We especially enjoyed the years when we all celebrated Thanksgiving and Oktoberfest together. All of the adults, at one time or another, were guilty of drinking too much beer on these occasions. Bob's mother was a devoted wife, loving mother, and fabulous cook. She passed away in 1991.

With my mother, Grace.

In 1993, with my mother's health continuing to go downhill, W.A. and Patsy moved into the house to take care of her. Their sons, David and Daniel, remained at their home, which was only two doors down from Mother's house. Unfortunately, Mother fell a couple times, which resulted in broken bones, and she was ordered to the Heritage Nursing facility.

When Mother was on her deathbed, she began to stare intently at the ceiling. I asked, "Are you OK, Mother?"

"Yes," she said. "I was just wondering if your father will recognize me when I get up there."

"Oh, sure he will." I snickered quietly to myself. Did she really think he would be up there? "Mother, it will not only be Daddy waiting for you but also your mother and father, Betty, and all of the people you loved so much."

It was that moment when I realized it wouldn't be long before she left this earth, bound for heaven. It felt like a knife had ripped my heart open, and standing there was a child—vulnerable, lost, and terribly afraid.

I cried out, "Oh, please, Mother, don't leave me behind. What will I do without you?"

Then, I crawled onto the bed and lay beside her, hugging her and kissing her face. Mother had a remarkable ability to never question God's will for her life. A rare quality few people have. She was all forgiving and always filled with amazing grace. She passed away peacefully a few hours later in the company of her family.

A few weeks later, my sister Vera and I were going through her things. We found a small green makeup bag, worn at the seams as if it had seen better days a long time ago. Mother hadn't worn makeup in many years, and we were surprised that she still had one. Vera unzipped the bag and reached inside. The first thing we found was an old lipstick, followed by a square compact and then a little, black address book with a photograph inside of my father with another woman. In the bottom was a big, black pocketknife.

"What is this?" Vera asked.

As I looked at this cold, black object, my heart stopped. I couldn't breathe. My eyes started to fill with tears. This was the knife my father had stabbed my mother with back when I was in high school. The pain all came back, and flashes of that night ran through my head so fast it was almost a blur. I couldn't speak. This was Daddy's hunting knife. Wow! I hadn't seen it in years. Why had she kept these awful things?

At the time that the stabbing took place, Vera lived in California with her husband, Ron, and her little baby son, Marty. She didn't know much about the incident. And she probably didn't recognize that this was the actual knife Daddy stabbed Mother with.

I asked Vera if it would be OK if I took the knife. She said it was fine with her but W.A. might want it. I thought, "He isn't getting this knife!" I took the makeup bag and the knife home that day.

Later, at home, I took the knife out of the bag and held it, sliding the cold, black object from one hand to the other. There was the little slot where your fingernail pulled the blade out. Should I open it? After much hesitation, I slowly drew out the long, sharp steel blade. I held it to my stomach. Then I held it to my side, seeing that it was long enough to go from one side of my body right through to the other side. Oh, what an awful thing! My poor, dear mother. Oh God. How terribly close she came to losing her life that night.

From the stabbing incident on, I had lost all respect and love for my father, and he knew it. I had also gained huge respect, if not understanding, for my mother's ability to forgive him. How could my father do such a thing? And how, for heaven's sake, could she have continued to live with him all those years afterward?

Daddy had quit drinking in 1962 after I married and left home. Mother and Daddy had fourteen good years together before he died, during which he was loving and attentive to her. She loved him and had never given up on him. She recognized that deep inside he was a good person, and she kept striving to love the good. They do say that, in the end, love conquers all. Who was I to question how she continued to live as she did? I folded the knife back up and placed it back into the little green coffin. Maybe one day, with God's help, I would find a way to forgive him. Deep in my heart, I was beginning to realize that I needed to do this, not for my father's sake but for mine.

It was in 1994 that Bob and I moved from Kitchener to Duntroon, a quaint little town near Collingwood, Ontario, where we bought our farm. It had a Victorian Gothic, redbrick farmhouse and a barn. It would take several years to restore both buildings to their original beauty.

Now was my opportunity to have a horse and learn to ride. I made up for the times that I spent sitting on the fence watching my childhood friend, Sylvia, ride at Sea Island Stables. I rode hunt seat, or what the British call English hunter saddle. It took many, many hours of lessons. I was fortunate to have owned three different and most wonderful horses. I really loved riding and had many great experiences. My riding career ended when I broke my sacrum and pelvis jumping with my horse.

While convalescing, I started renewing my love for art. I read many art history books and eventually began painting again, and I haven't stopped since. I used to joke that I was saving painting for my old age, and guess what? Here I am!

In January 1999, during a routine physical, Bob's doctors discovered he had terminal prostate cancer. The cancer had already spread, and treatment started immediately. His diagnosis wasn't good. He was told, in a round-about way, that he would have only three to four years to live.

Through a friend, Bob contacted Memorial Sloan Kettering Cancer Center in New York City, where he signed up to be a participant in prostate research. He made a commitment that he would give himself and his resources to helping find a cure for prostate cancer. He honored it to the end.

We began to travel extensively all over the world. Bob soon fulfilled one bucket list and started another. He joked with me that maybe I should start working on *my* bucket list also. We took some unbelievable trips to the Great Wall of China, the Hermitage in Russia, France, Italy, and many other countries around the world. Rather than concentrate on his disease and think about dying, Bob embraced living.

Bob's father, Frank, was a prince of a guy who always loved a good joke. Times had been very difficult for him since Vera passed away. But even though he mourned the loss of his lifetime sweetheart, his sense of humor carried him through. Frank died in 2002, surrounded by his family.

Eliza's Last Days (2004–2013)

In early May 2004, I stopped in to visit with Eliza at her home. On my visits I usually gave her a little pocket money, and we always enjoyed our little chats about old times.

When I knocked on the door, Eliza's sister Louise opened it and told me that Eliza was now in Magnolia Manor Nursing Home. She said that if I wanted to see her, I should go as soon as possible, because Eliza was going downhill fast.

I immediately drove to the nursing home. I went to the front desk, where I got directions to Eliza's room. I walked down a long hallway, and I started reading the nameplates of the patients that were on the doors. Eliza was here with some of Sea Island's and St. Simons's most prominent citizens. My goodness, Eliza was in high cotton with these folk. There was no class distinction here.

When I walked into the room, she was lying there staring into space. My heart just sank.

"Hi, Eliza; it's Carol." No response.

"Eliza, hey, it's Carol! You remember me—your baby Carol Jane." Still no response.

"You remember W.A., don't you?" A slight movement. "You know. You remember W.A."

She sat straight up in bed and muttered, "Oh Lord, that child! That devil child." Eliza lay back down, and I thought she might have had a heart attack and died. I was at a loss for words, holding her hand as tears streamed down my face. She didn't respond to me. I kissed her on the cheek and said good-bye. As I walked out of the nursing home, I could hardly see. I sat in my car crying, knowing that I would never see her again.

I loved you, Eliza. I truly did. I hated to see you go. We had such great times together. You had so little and gave so much. I'm proud that you were my friend.

Later, after I returned to Canada, I was saddened to hear that Eliza had passed away. Over the next few years, whenever I went to St. Simons, I stopped at Louise's house to pay my respects, but no matter how many times I went there, I couldn't catch anyone at home. I left several notes and never got a response to any of them.

One day I was driving by Eliza's old house, and a car was backing out of the driveway. I quickly pulled in. It was Eliza's grandniece. I asked if her grandmother, Louise, was at home. She informed me that Louise had passed away a few months short of her ninetieth birthday. This news was a total shock since I had visited her just before Eliza had passed away. I asked where Eliza and Louise were buried, and she told me they were in the slave cemetery at Sea Island Golf Club, where only the descendants of the Retreat Plantation slaves could be interred. It was a very emotional moment for me. I explained they had been beloved friends of our family and I wanted to pay my respects.

I left Proctor Lane and drove to the cemetery at Sea Island Golf Club. I wandered in and out of the graves and immediately spotted Neptune Small's headstone. I continued looking for Eliza's and Louise's headstones. First I found Louise White Butler and then Eliza's father, Floyd, and his wife, Ellen. I wandered around some more and spotted the headstones for Victoria, Eliza's grandmother, and then Jupiter, her grandfather who was a slave from Postell of Kelvin Grove Plantation. Unfortunately there were so many unmarked graves there that I had no clue which one was Eliza's.

During the weeks to come, I kept trying to catch the grandniece to see if she would help me locate it, but I was never able to catch her at home. A few weeks later, determined to find my friend, I returned to the cemetery, where I made a full chart of the location of each and every grave in the cemetery, but I still couldn't find Eliza's. I knew she was buried here in this cemetery somewhere, and I was going to find her, come hell or high water! At this point in time, I just didn't know how.

Love and Loss

During each of the next three years, at least one of my most beloved passed away. Each loss carried me through waves of pain, sadness, and grief, but each time, I strove to find comfort in the knowledge that death merely places a temporary curtain between us. For every measure of sadness I felt, I realized there was an infinite quantity of love between us that could never die. I felt grateful they had played such large parts in my life, and I was certain we would all be together again.

April 30, 2009

My sister Vera had moved to Texas, where she lived with her son Martin and his family. On my last visit with her, she told me that the days spent with her grandchildren were the best days of her life. I was so happy for her. She deserved that happy time more than anyone I knew. When you grow up as children in a traumatic or extremely difficult environment, you form an extra-special connection that goes beyond the usual closeness of siblings. You have to support each other and care for each other in order just to survive. It's a bond that can never be broken.

Vera passed away on a beautiful spring day. I remembered how she used to let me sleep with my bed beneath the window of our stifling room. I would lay there watching stars appear and disappear between the oak-tree branches, and I'd feel connected to the heavens. All the while Vera, who sacrificed her comfort for mine, suffered the kitchen heat and summer humidity without complaint so that I could breathe. She saved my life more than once with her quick thought and actions. What a beautiful person she was, and how lucky I had been to have her as my sister.

January 28, 2011

I adored my brother, and there were plenty of times when I hated my brother. I saw him at his best, and I saw him at his worst. The struggle to survive Daddy's binges and behavior was different for him than it was for us girls, but no less difficult and often much lonelier. W.A. and I did have a period of time where we were distant from each other, but, thank God, we were back to acting like it was the old times before he passed away. When I think back to that boy who put up with his little sister tagging along and the numerous times he protected me from bullies or taught me what I needed to know, I realize how lucky I was to have him for a brother. I was so proud of him. He was my hero, and I loved him dearly.

July 22, 2012

God did answer my prayers that Sunday at church many years ago. When I asked him to bring me a new husband, he brought Bob into my life. It took me a long time to accept that God does hear you even though you may not think so. You just have to give him a little time to help you in your life. With the hindsight one gains from a lifetime of experience, I can honestly say I have never been disappointed. Everything I needed came to me in its own good time—God's time.

So, how do you write about thirty-one years of marriage? God blessed Bob and me with our family and with the joy of beautiful, healthy grandchildren. Bob was a wonderful husband. He was my protector, guarding me from the fears and pain of my past. He was gentle and kind, and he never displayed anger. He always practiced patience, even when I challenged him.

I gave Bob my heart, body, and soul. I cared for his needs whether he was sick or healthy. I devoted my energy and time to helping him and doing fun things together, and I respected his desire to have his own space when he needed it. We shared our hopes, prayers, and dreams. I respected him for his accomplishments, but mostly for his character as a man.

Bob had always been courageous, but his last battle became an inspiration to us all. "Why should I stop living?" he'd ask me with a smile on his face. "I'm not dead yet." He never complained about his disease or his treatment, and he kept his zest for life to the end. I'm convinced it was that zest for life and his positive attitude that kept him going long past the two to three-year expiry date given to him by the oncologist. He outlived his sentence by ten years, and well-lived years they were.

Bob loved his children and grandchildren more than they will ever know, and he was so grateful that, in his last week of life, he was surrounded by his family at our farm in Duntroon. When he passed, I felt like I'd lost my best friend. No words can ever truly capture the emptiness of loss or describe how the knowledge that we would meet again offers little comfort from the pain of grief. It is true what they say about grief being a process, though I prefer to think of it as just a small part of a path that we all walk.

Before Bob passed away, he requested several things. He wanted to be buried in Georgia, he asked that I be buried next to him if that was all right with me, and he asked that I have a fantabulous wake in both Canada and in Georgia. He told me that he didn't want it to be a sad event, but a celebration of life.

Chapter 30

MAKING THINGS RIGHT—2013

ou would think I'd had enough to do with death, graves, and memorials after losing so many dear ones in three short years, but I still had one more thing to do. This unfinished business had been bothering me ever since I tried to find Eliza's grave in 2005. It was about time I found out where she was.

As soon as I returned to St. Simons from Canada, I went over to Hall, Jones and Brown Funeral Home in Brunswick to make inquiries as to Eliza's whereabouts. This was the second time I had stopped in to see them, and I came out with the same result as before. They could not answer my query. I returned for the third time with my chart in hand, determined to find the location of Eliza's grave.

The lady in the funeral home office was a very attractive black woman. I'd guess she was about forty years old, and she reigned supreme over that office. I unfolded my chart, which was made up of at least eight sheets of paper taped together in all directions. I placed it on her desk and gave her "the look." Then she gave me "the look." Our eyes met in the middle. I leaned over, closer to her, and I pointed to the chart.

"You buried Eliza. Where?" A big toothy smile came over her face. She shook her head and laughed.

"OK. It's a lot of trouble, but we will find her." She got up from her desk and walked over to a closet, removing raincoats, umbrellas, and other miscellaneous items. Stepping further into the closet, she opened a file cabinet drawer and started flipping through the files.

Suddenly she cried out, "Yep, we found her!" She walked over to the desk while reading the contents of the file and then looked down at my chart and, with her finger almost brushing against my nose, pointed to a specific spot on the chart.

"That's her—right there." I let out a deep sigh of relief. Eliza was in one of the unmarked graves.

"How could Eliza be in an unmarked grave?"

"Looks like no one bought her a permanent headstone. Sometimes the original marker that designates who is buried there goes missing."

Eliza impacted my life in such a beautiful way; I now hoped I could do something for her in return. I thanked the lady, turned and rushed out of the door to my car, sped across the causeway to the Sea Island Golf Club, and hightailed it to the cemetery. Having spent so much time creating my chart, I knew exactly where I was going. Passing headstones and markers, I quickly made my way to a lonely, unmarked grave.

"Eliza, you once were lost, and now you are found! I promise you this day that you will have a proper headstone, if it's the last thing I do."

In the fall of 2013, I made an appointment with Eliza's niece to go to the funeral home and choose a headstone. We were going over the details when Arlene mentioned Eliza's two sons who had predeceased her.

"What? Two sons? You must be mistaken. Eliza didn't have any children."

"When Eliza was twelve years old," Arlene explained, "she had a boy named Alfred. Her sister Louise raised him. At fifteen, she had a second son, Willie, and he was raised by Eliza's brother, Simon." At that point Arlene handed me a photo of Eliza and then some old, old pages that looked like parchment and were the inventory lists from Retreat Plantation showing their ancestors' names, ages, and values.

I froze. I couldn't even speak. Twelve. Fifteen. So many thoughts ran through my mind. I could only imagine what she had been through, and I was certain it hadn't been by choice. I was completely devastated that such a thing had happened to her at such a young age. Looking at those inventory pages, I almost felt sick to think that our forefathers had been a part of something so despicable. (See appendix.)

I'm sure that Mother knew all about this, but I never heard a word of it. Now I understood about those emotional conversations in the kitchen between Mother and Eliza so long ago. I felt like someone had just stabbed me in my heart. I saw her in a totally new light. Oh, my poor Eliza! When she became a mother, she was only a child herself. Now I understood her attraction to all little children. She had missed the opportunity to raise her own; perhaps that was why her love overflowed to others.

I could hardly speak to Denita, the secretary at the funeral home, when I finalized the order for Eliza's headstone. For days I was overcome with feelings of anguish and empathy.

It was some weeks later that Arlene told me Eliza's son Willie died in Atlanta, leaving behind his wife, Rosalind; two sons; and several grandchildren. Rosalind had moved back to St. Simons and was now working at Sea Island. That Eliza had left a legacy of her own descendants was the most wonderful news. I couldn't wait to meet Eliza's daughter-in-law and grandchildren. Arlene gave me her number, and it wasn't long before I called her. What a thrill to be able to tell Rosalind about the wonderful role Eliza had played in my life and to hear so much more from Roz about Eliza's family. Ensuring that a gravestone was placed to honor Eliza had turned into a much bigger event. Now her descendants for generations to come would be able to visit her and know something of this wonderful woman whose heart had blessed us all.

Chapter 31

FREE AT LAST—JANUARY 27, 2014

*T*wo months later, I received a telephone call from Denita saying Eliza's grave marker was being delivered to the cemetery. I telephoned Eliza's daughter-in-law Rosalind and asked her to meet me at the cemetery on Sunday.

Then, on Sunday after church, I left my house in German Village and drove south on Lawrence Road, stopping at the Oglethorpe Memorial Gardens cemetery. Getting out of the car, I walked through thick, spongy wet grass to where my family members were buried. As I stood at the base of Bob's grave, I suddenly laughed.

"I see you are still reserving a spot for me! Oh, good—there's no expiration date on it." There is something chilling about seeing your name on a grave marker. I had forgotten that my name and birth date had been engraved next to Bob's when he passed away.

"Sweetheart, I gave you three chances to change your mind about being buried here with my redneck family. And every time you made the same comment: 'It would be an honor and a privilege to be buried here with your family.' I just hope you know I appreciated that. I loved you so very much."

I then walked over to my parents' graves. I found myself telling them about my memoir and how hard it had been to write about the struggles I'd had over the years. One of the hardest things I'd had to face was my inability to forgive my father.

"It kept me shackled to you, Daddy. For so long, my unforgiving heart robbed me of joy. When I started writing about you and all those things you did, I cried so hard; I cried for Mother and for each one of us, including myself. But one day, through the gift of grace, I found myself crying for you. I forgive you, Daddy. I really mean this. I forgive you."

Chilled by the cool air, I started trembling as I rushed back to my car. I climbed into the driver's seat and rested my head on the steering wheel. Tears flowed down my face, while a sensation of peace washed over me. I felt suddenly so light, as if something terribly dark and heavy had been lifted from me.

Collecting my thoughts as I left the cemetery, I drove to the intersection of Frederica and Sea Island Roads and sat at the traffic light, waiting for it to turn green. My attention was drawn to the spot where the Sea Island Stables used to be. I had a vision of my friend Sylvia prancing around the ring on her horse, only this time I was riding along with her.

The light changed, and I continued south through heavy traffic. I passed by the spot where Pete's Place and the Oasis once stood. Another vision came to me of a young girl bursting from the bar and running like hell to reach home so she could tell her mother, "Daddy's coming."

Circling the roundabout at Demere, I passed the slave cabin, now called the Tabby House. Here I could see Eliza with the other children dancing in the yard for the tourists. I wished I could have joined in with them. It would have been such fun.

Further down where the airport landing runway ran alongside the road, I envisioned fields of fine Sea Island cotton and slaves with long burlap sacks tied over their shoulders, working hard in the hot sun. I was driving on a road that had been built by the toil of slaves. Originally, this road was lined with about five hundred trees and was part of the Avenue of Oaks. Carriages and wagons drawn by teams of horses used to transport their precious cargo of cotton and slaves where I was now driving in my car in comfort.

Passing through the only section of the Avenue of Oaks that still exist-ed, I turned right and looked over my shoulder across St. Simons Sound to Jekyll Island. One hundred and fifty years ago, a ship called *The Wanderer* smuggled the last documented slave cargo to the United States, closing the era of slave trading. Only 409 of the 500 people who had been forced, in shackles, to board the ship survived the trip to Jekyll.

As I passed the ruins of the Retreat Hospital, I thought of the births and deaths of the slaves. My heart broke when I thought about the high mortality rate of the newborn babies, not only those born into slavery but also those of the slaves' masters as well. Anna Matilda King was the only child of William and Hannah Page's ten children to survive to adulthood. Upon reaching the Sea Island Golf Club, I parked in front of a building that was once the corn barn for the Retreat Plantation. I looked up to see Roz and two handsome young men walking toward me. She walked over and introduced me to her sons, Rodney and Willie. I was just thrilled that Eliza's grandsons had joined us. I was sad to see that Eliza's niece, Arlene, was not with them. They explained that she was ill and unfortunately was unable to join us. Without her help, this wonderful day would not have happened. In my hands were a dozen colorful roses, and I gave a couple to each person. We walked over, excited to see Eliza's marker, and we each placed a rose on her grave. It was a very emotional time as tears trickled down my cheek. It was final. There she was, my sweet Eliza. I had found her, and now I could rest knowing that she would never be lost or forgot-ten over time.

We all walked over to the grave of Eliza's sister Louise, where we placed more roses. We continued walking through the slave cemetery. Then, I pointed out Victoria's marker (who was their great-great grandmother). She was born on Retreat Plantation. The young men were touched and I think a little overwhelmed by the realization of it all. We all walked back and gathered around Eliza's grave. I asked if I could say something be-fore we left. We bowed our heads, and I said, "Eliza, you comforted me when my mother was sick. You brought laughter, joy, and friendship to our house. You may have seemed less than perfect in some people's eyes, but to me, God could not have molded a more perfect person. This marker is a testament to you, to your ancestors who suffered for so long, and to your descendants for generations to come. Let us *all* not be slaves to our past."

Carol Hamby

I have a dream that one day on the red hills of Georgia, the sons of former slaves and the sons of former slave owners will be able to sit down together at the table of brotherhood. Free at last! Free at last! Thank God Almighty, we are free at last!

Speech by Dr. Martin Luther King Jr.
Delivered 28 August 1963,
Lincoln Memorial, Washington, DC

APPENDIX

Appraisement of Estate of Anna Matilda King
Inventory of the Estate of Mrs. Anna Matilda King

Retreat and Newfield Plantation				Acres
Land and Buildings:				
First Quality Hammock Land				250
Second	"	"	"	261
Scrub and Pine				804
Savannah and Pond				110
Marsh				650
				2075

7200 Pounds Cotton at 7 _____ per pound $5040.

No.	Negroes	Ages	Valuation
1	Abram	43	$800.
2	Alick Boyd	47	800.
3	Ellen	43	500.
4	Jennett	21	1000.
5	Hannah	17	400.
6	Charlotte	14	900.
7	Julia	11	600.
8	Abel	8	500.
9	Patience	4	300.

10	Alick)	33	1000.
11	Delia)	23	1000.
12	Charles Jr.)	28	1000.
13	Lucinda)	26	1000.
14	Alick	5	300.
15	Alfred)	37	1000.
16	Liddy)	56	600.
17	Frederick	16	700.
18	Adeleth	12	500.
19	Abner	39	900.
20	Sander	32	1000.
21	Rathley's Betty	22	1000.
22	Nancy	2	200.
23	Boney)	45	800.
24	Sarah)	35	900.
25	Toby	13	600.
26	Albert	6	400.
27	Ned .	3	200.
28	Margaret	3	200.
29	Hetty	0.4	100.
30	Clementine	46	700.
31	Middleton	22	1000.
32	Christianna and child)	20	1000.
33	Theresa)	1	200.
34	Isabel	13	800.
35	Justine	3	200.
36	Ishmael	31	1000.
37	Frank	21	800.
38	Clementine, Jr.	23	800.
39	Binah	3	200.
40	Jerry	40	900.
41	Edinborough- no value	27	000.
42	Hercules	62	200.

43	Laura)	40	700.
44	Singleton)	2	200.
45	Jimmy	36	900.
46	Sam	30	1000.
47	Jimper)	30	1000.
48	Linda)	23	1000.
49	Joe)	34	1000.
50	Ruthy)	31	900.
51	Dawson	5	250.
52	June	3	200.
53	Julian	1	200.
54	Lady no value	73	000.
55	Quamina	65	100.
56	John)	34	1000.
57	Betty)	30	1000.
58	Louisa	8	600.
59	Marcia	4	250.
60	Quamina	2	200.
61	John	0.8	100.
62	Mack)	35	1000.
63	Amy)	34	1000.
64	Ella	14	900.
65	Jane	5	350.
66	Lonzo	0.5	100.
67	March)	53	700.
68	Peggy)	46	500.
69	Jack	28	1000.
70	Jimmy	21	1000.
71	Matilda	17	1000.
72	Cilla	14	900.
73	Maria	12	800.
74	Nelly	9	450.
75	Abigail	4	250.
76	Maria	42	850.
77	Tilla and)	19	1000.
78	Child Anne)	0.3	100.

79	Emily	15	900.
80	Henry	13	600.
81	Augusta	4	250.
82	Herbert	0.3	100.
83	Big Peter) no value	76	000.
84	Polly)	58	150.
85	Nella)	38	800.
86	Flora)	41	700.
87	Lizzy	13	900.
88	Henrietta	10	550.
89	Anthony	8	450.
90	Hercules	5	300.
91	Ferdinand	3	250.
92	Ned	38	1000.
93	Patience	36	200.
94	Clara	17	1000.
95	Rhina	33	1000.
96	Peter	32	1000.
97	Pussy	65	200.
98	Charles	41	700.
99	Neptune)	28	1000.
100	Illa)	25	1000.
101	Leonora	0.3	100.
102	George)	38	1000.
103	Sukey)	29	1000.
104	Camilla	11	600.
105	Modina	9	500.
106	Cornelia	2	200.
107	Alice	1	100.
108	Robert)	23	1000.
109	Julianna)	25	1000.
110	Balaam	7	400.
111	Mina	4	250.
112	Enick	0.4	100.

113	Richard)	49	500. *Eliza's Great Grandfather*
114	Nancy)	40	500. *"Great Grandmother*
115	Richard Jr.	19	1000. *Child of Richard & Nancy*
116	Mary	17	1000. " " "
117	Elizabeth	15	1000. " " "
118	Ansel	14	700. " " "
119	Gabriel	11	500. " " "
120	Victoria	10	500. *Eliza's Grandmother*
121	Nathaniel	5	350. *Child of Richard & Nancy*
122	Harper	5	350. " " "
123	Thomas	2	200. " " "
124	Rose	45	600.
125	William	23	1000.
126	Caeser	21	1000.
127	Siah	13	600.
128	Rosa	13	600.
129	Mary	9	400.
130	Joseph	7	350.
131	Toney)	51	1000.
132	Jane)	39	800.
133	Bella	20	1000.
134	Jane	10	500.
135	Toney Jr.	5	350.
136	Sally	2	200.
137	William)	37	1000.
138	Pleasant)	19	1000.
139	Dorinda	0.6	100.
140	William	10	500.
141	John	10	500.
142	Adam	8	400.

Carol Hamby

No.	Plantation Provisions	Valuation
1240	Bushels of Corn in Barn	1240.
20	Bushels of Pease	20.
1	Lot of Fodder	<u>50.</u>
		(Total 1310.)

No.	Plantation Provisions	Valuation
1	Timber Cart	75.
1	Horse Cart	20.
1	Small Wagon	10.
1	Lot of Carpenters Tools & Grindstone	35.
1	Lot of Blacksmiths Tools & Iron	20.
8	Axes, Plows and Sweeps and Schools	109.
17	Ox Chains	25.50
20	Trace Chains	3.75
5	Wheel Barrows 2.50, 7 Sythes 7.00	9.50
12	Forks 3.00, 16 Shovels 8.00	11.00
11	Spades 5.50, 2 Sugar Boilers 25.00	30.50
1	Corn Sheller 10.00, 4 Cart ___90.00	<u>100.00</u>
		(Total 449.25)

Carriages & c.

1 new carriage 300.00, 1 Old Ditto 30.00	$330.00
2 Sets of Harness, Old $5.00, New $35	40.00
1 Worn Carriage Frame	5.00
3 Rack Frames	15.00
3 Cow Hides	7.50

Horses

No.		Valuation
1	Betsey	$175.00
1	Kickapoo	150.00
2	Black Kate & Colt – 9 mos. old	90.00
2	Weldon " " " " "	100.00
2	Kate and Colt – 21 mos. old	45.00
1	Porpoise	45.00

1	McVaroy	40.00
1	Louisa	50.00
1	Tilla	<u>50.00</u>

(Total $750.00)

Cattle

| 37 | Oxen, 6 Steers, 12 Yearlings, 17 Milk Cows, 4 Calves | $750.00 |
| 30 | Hogs | <u>60.00</u> |

(Total $810.00)

Poultry

| 26 | Ducks 9.75, 13 Guina Fowls 3.25 | $10.00 |
| 46 | Fowls 11.50, 55 Turkeys 41.25, 4 Geese 3.00 | <u>55.75</u> |

(Total $65.75)

Furniture

.9 common carpets, 1 brussels ditto, 2 rugs, 2 mats, 3 hair sofas, 1 centra table, 2 small ditto, 1 book case, 1 old set of stands, 1 new set of stands, 12 oak chairs, 4 ottomans, 1 shell case, 3 Etageres, 3 couches, 2 sick chairs, 2 camp chairs, 1 velvet rocking chair, 3 parlor chairs, 12 framed engravings, 2 flower pots, 1 _____ case, 1 small, 1 breakfast ditto, 1 small round ditto, 1 side board, 1 fire screen, 1 refrigerator, 10 window curtains, 2 clocks, 1 entry lamp, 4 Kerosine lamps, 2 oil ditto, 2 large fluid ditto, 1 small fluid lamp, 4 Wash tubs, 8 cedar buckets,12 smoothing irons, 2 bath tubs, 2 safes, 6 andirons (pairs), 2 fenders, 8 pitchers, 10 basin, 6 Wash Stands, 3 brooms.

Kitchen and Dairy Utensils

7 pots, 1 digester, 2 kettles, 3 ovens, 1 large pot, 1 coffee mill, 1 spider, 1 cullender, 1 serve, 1 spice grinder, 1 grater, 1 sausage stuffer, 2 pine tables, 14 milk pans, 4 pie pans, 8 feather beds, 11 mattresses, 8 bolsters, 13 pillows, 9 comfors, 13 blankets, 7 quilts, 10 pairs linen sheets, 8 prs. Cotton sheets, 12 prs. linen pillow cases, 15 pr. Cotton ditto, 4 pair linen bolster cases, 5 pair cotton ditto, 13 Table Cloths, 4 Colored table clothes, 39 hand towels, 24 pantry ditto, 36 table napkins, 12 colored napkins, 12 Bed steads, 1 plate,

warmer, 48 self-sealing cans, 12 grass mats for the table, 12 cotton mats for the table, 1 set of dish covers, 36 table knives, 9 carving forks, 6 waiters

House and kitchen furniture valuation $1750

No.	Silver
30	large forks, 28 small ditto, 18 table spoons, 18 desert ditto, 18 tea spoons.
18	fruit knives, 2 custard spoons, 2 sauce ladles
4	salt spoons, 1 mustard spoon, 1 fish knife, 2 butter knives
1	sugar tongs, 1 soup ladle, 1 old spoon, 2 water pitchers.
1	cordial stand, 4 salt stands, 1 sugar dish.
1	sugar sprinkler, 1 cream pot.

No.	Plate Silver
4	fruit baskets, 4 decanter stands, 2 salvers, 1 urn
1	caster stand

Silver & Plate Valuation $1000.

China Glass

1 entire set of fine dinner china, 60 plates, 20 dishes of common china, 4 tureen, 26 tumblers, 78 wine glasses, 12 egg glasses, 11 decanters, 18 finger bowls, 2 cut glass dishes, 4 glass preserve saucers, 21 tea plates, 1 Tea Pot, 1 milk ditto, 5 bowls, 18 glass goblets.

Valuation $175.00

(Total value of everything not including land $82,392.50)

(State of Georgia Glynn County)

We do certify upon oath that as far as was foregoing contains a true appraisement of the goods, Chattels and credit of the Estate of Mrs. Anna Matilda King deceased, to the best of our judgment and conditioning. Given under our hands and Official Signatures this 11th day of January 1860.

W. Dart)
Alix Scranton)
Horace B. Gould) Appraisers
Charles L. Schlatter

I do certify that the above appraisers were sworn to perform their duty as appraisers according (to) Law, this 11th day of January 1860.
James Postell, J.P.

Recorded this 24th day of February 1860.
Stephen J. Gorton, Ordinary

ACKNOWLEDGEMENTS

I would like to give special thanks to Lorraine O'Donnell Williams, who inspired me to write this book, and to my friend, Petra Travers, who gave me a wealth of encouragement. Also, thanks to Elaine Deaver for her support in transcribing all my notes. Elaine was of major help to me while she typed out the manuscript. She listened to my stories and gave me feedback. She encouraged me, laughed with me, and cried with me. Without her by my side, this book may never have been completed. And finally, thank you to the most gifted editor and freelance writer an author could ever hope to find, Cynthia J Hurn. Her passion for writing stories that touch the heart and her skilled understanding of the writer's craft brought this memoir to life.